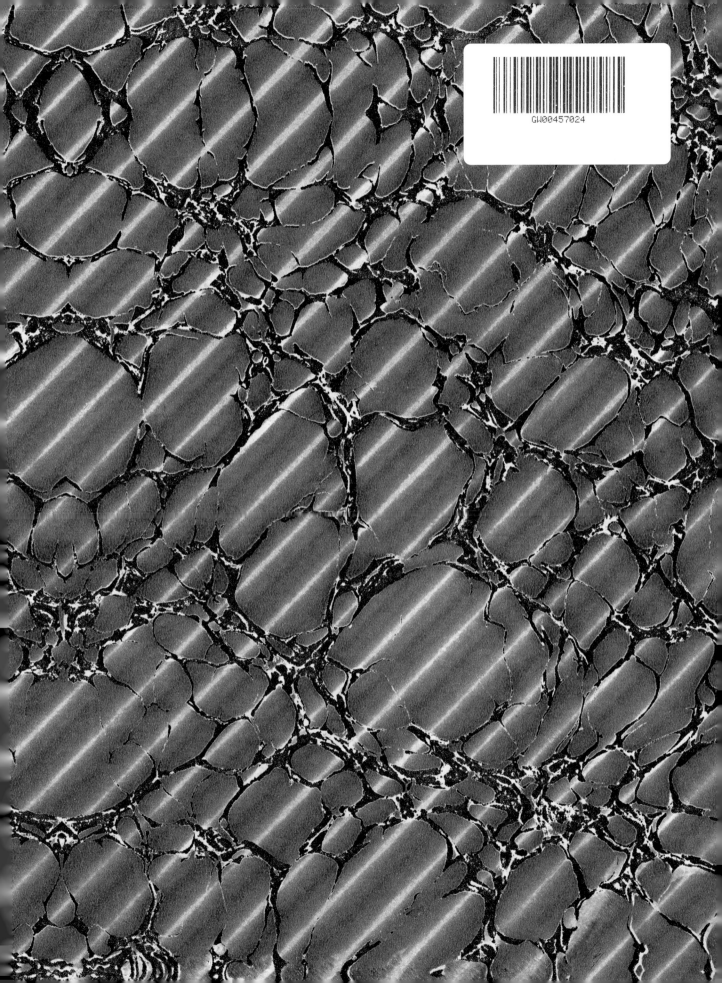

YESTERDAY'S TOWN: CHESHAM

FRONT COVER: Market Square, Chesham, c.1920 — long before the Market Hall made way for the motorcar.

*The great wheel of Lords Mill, Waterside is still, as a Victorian
lad contemplates the Chess. Here is the essence of Chesham,
a working town since the Saxons diverted the river and
built the mills.*

YESTERDAY'S TOWN
CHESHAM

A MEDLEY OF MEMORY
AND FACT IN THE EYE
OF THE PAST
BY

CLIVE BIRCH
AND
JOHN ARMISTEAD

BARRACUDA BOOKS LIMITED
CHESHAM BUCKINGHAMSHIRE
MCMLXXVII

PUBLISHED BY BARRACUDA BOOKS LIMITED
CHESHAM, ENGLAND
AND PRINTED BY
FRANK ROOK LIMITED
TOWER BRIDGE ROAD
LONDON SE1

BOUND BY
LEIGHTON-STRAKER BOOKBINDING CO. LTD.
LONDON NW10

JACKET PRINTED BY
WHITE CRESCENT PRESS LIMITED
LUTON, ENGLAND

LITHOGRAPHY BY
SOUTH MIDLANDS LITHOPLATES LIMITED
LUTON, ENGLAND

TYPE SET IN 11pt PRESS ROMAN
BY BEAVER REPROGRAPHICS LIMITED
BUSHEY, ENGLAND
©Clive Birch & John Armistead

CONTENTS

ACKNOWLEDGEMENTS

We would thank firstly Ray East, without whose enquiring mind and courtesy many of these pictures would never have gone onto film, but died with their owners. We thank him for allowing us access to his collection and for his enthusiasm for the project. In doing so, we also pay tribute to his namesakes who took some of the pictures of the past, but especially to W. Butts, Chesham's master cameraman, many of whose photographs are here. He was the Francis Frith of Chesham, though that gentleman is also represented, thanks to our friend John Buck who runs the Collection and has allowed us the unique privilege of reproduction in book form of some originals.

Secondly, we would pay tribute to the town's established historians — Arnold H. J. Baines and H. Stanley Cox. Arnold and Stan are old friends, and have advised and helped us both; their memories and knowledge are legion and we are in their debt.

Thirdly, our thanks go to all those who have offered and given help and material for this book; among them Frank White, William Birch, Percy Birtchnell, Caroline Copperwaite (nee Climpson), Charles Darvell and all those acknowledged in the captions, and to Bernard Edwards, editor of *The Amersham & Chesham Advertiser,* Dr. Dennis Rhodes, asst. Keeper of Printed Books, at the British Library, and Reading Room Superintendent Mr. Goossens at the Newspaper Library, for last minute research and facilities as the book went to press.

We are grateful too to Tony White and the management of the *Bucks Examiner* for readily allowing access to the paper's old files, and to Ken Crabb of Chapter One bookshop for his essential enthusiasm and constructive support for this project from its inception.

Finally, our families and friends have taken a lively interest in this book and we hope they will like it as much as we have enjoyed putting it together.

Keys to caption letters, giving acknowledgement to those who have lent specific pictures.

FFC	Francis Frith Collection 1976
FW	Frank White
CC	Caroline Copperwaite
WR	Wilfred Reynolds
AJS	A. J. Stone
AS	Arthur Stratford
RC	Richard Chapman
CM/PB	County Museum / Percy Birtchnell
JPM	J. P. Mullett
RH	Mrs. R. Horsnell (nee Culverhouse)
IN	Mrs. Ivy Nash
DJN	D. J. Newton
MH	Miss Mabel Howard
CHD	Charles H. Darvell
NO	Norman Oakins
NL	Newspaper Library
GS	Mrs. G. Summerling
BE	Bernard Edwards

The decorative frames for the text pages were selected from the 1848 *Chesham Almanack.*

INTRODUCTION

The idea for this book was born of several separate incidents and conversations. Some time after *The Book of Chesham* had passed into a second edition, we asked ourselves what we were going to do with the many fascinating old photos excluded from that first published history of the town. Chesham's bookseller Ken Crabb often mentioned the steady stream of residents and visitors who asked for something less than a history and more than a guide-book. Historian associates and friends in the library service also suggested there was a place for an informed picture book of the past.

We decided to see just how many relevant illustrations we could put together. The final total — and they were still coming along when the book went to press — exceeded five hundred. We eliminated many of these because they lacked originality, were of poor quality or duplicated one another.

From the start, we agreed we would not just produce an unrelated series of old pictures, fun though that might be, and easy to compile. We wanted to offer an insight into Chesham as it was not so long ago; to bring back to life, albeit briefly, the Chesham which changed so little until the Second World War buried 'sleepy hollow', and the car, commuter and urban creep combined to open it up to the world.

We have taken a period roughly 1820 to 1920, with the emphasis on the turn of the century. The pictures represent a selection from private and public collections, and the text is culled from a variety of original and printed sources. Against convention, the book has been arranged with the pictures leading the text. Six aspects of the town surround four brief, self-contained 'essays' on related matters, and the middle of the book is devoted to a selection of strange, curious, or significant items which we found intriguing and entertaining. Generally speaking, there has been no attempt at chronology with the pictures, but they are logically grouped within each section. The first selection takes the reader round the town as a pedestrian interested in the past, the second separates sport from public affairs or matters military, the third groups denominations, the fourth projects a monumental pub crawl through the past and the fifth takes the town's industry first and its commerce last. The final section looks at coach, carriage, railway and motor.

The four main chapters look at the town circa 1900, the private and public purse, pubs, and communications. The material within 'Small Matter' covers the century by decades as far as sources allow.

Overall, we hope this book will complement and supplement *The Book of Chesham* for those who have it; will lead others to an interest in the town's past; will amuse and entertain as well as inform newcomers and visitors; will instruct younger readers without boring them and will serve as a pleasant reflection of a pleasant town.

Dedication

For Raymond Birch, CBE,
Albert and Nellie Armistead,
and for Valerie Baskwill,
who remember the past.

SOURCES

For the student, the main sources for this particular book are as follows:—

Chesham Almanacks for 1845-8 (Author's and H. Stanley Cox collections).
Kelly's Directories, 1864, 1889 (Author's collection)*
Chesham Recorder 1868 (Percy Birtchnell collection)
Chesham News 1876/7 and 1887 (Percy Birtchnell Collection)
Tithe map and assessment, 1842 (Public Record Office, Asheridge repository)
The Chesham Advertiser 1892-3; The Chesham and Bucks Examiners 1889-1920 (British Museum Newspaper Library, and Bucks Examiner, Chesham)
The Chesham News, The Bucks Recorder, the Mid-Bucks News (Newspaper Library).

*Note: Other directories are available at The Buckingham Collection, County Library, Aylesbury

For this period, there are many useful documents in the County Record Office at Aylesbury, and information within local church registers, and material held by the Chess Valley Archaeological and Historical Society.

BIBLIOGRAPHY

There are not many books available specific to Chesham. The following may be found useful in a direct or related way.

Discovering Chesham by Val Biro with historical notes by Arnold Baines
The Book of Chesham by Clive Birch
The Book of Aylesbury by Clive Birch
The Book of Hemel Hempstead and Berkhamsted by Gwennah Robinson
Bygone Berkhamsted by Percy Birtchnell
A Short History of Berkhamsted by Percy Birtchnell
History of Hemel Hempstead by members of the Hemel Hempstead Local History and Records Society
The Book of Amersham by L. Elgar Pike and Clive Birch
A History of Chesham Bois by L. Elgar Pike

ABOVE: On the Roman route to Chesham, Latimer must be one of the most pleasant curtain-raisers to any English town. Here the road into the village boasts no bridge – only a ford and a footbridge beneath the waterfall.
LEFT: The vanished church, that stood near the Chess at Latimer. BELOW: With Latimer road giving way to Waterside, the river wends its way beneath Lords Mill. (FFC).

ABOVE: Is this Climpson's horse pausing just below Lords Mill? BELOW: The cart sheds between the Mill and the long gone cottages, seen from an untidy Moor.

*ABOVE: Waterside cottages since replaced, by the watering
place below the Mill (NO) and BELOW: the path (now road)
past today's swimming pool.*

13

ABOVE: Shackman's is here now in Waterside and BELOW: the approach to the Pound has not changed much in fifty years.

14

ABOVE: New road lacked today's pretty woods, but BELOW: Amy (Amen) Mill serenely marked the gateway to the town, while RIGHT: The Minerals had yet to suffer fuel-pump blight.

*ABOVE: Recognise the site? It's Amy Mill pond, looking
towards The Forelands, Red Lion street, where
BELOW: traffic was light, and INSET: progress favoured the
bicycle and cart despite the improvised 'service station'
where the Dept. of Employment stands today, and Henry
Hearn kept his horses.*

16

ABOVE: Red Lion street corner, heavily advertised, presages
BELOW: Stratford's Yard, now reduced and isolated behind
bars in East street.

Two views of the old and then notorious Townfield
LEFT: between the Examiner building and the
house where the Embassy is today.

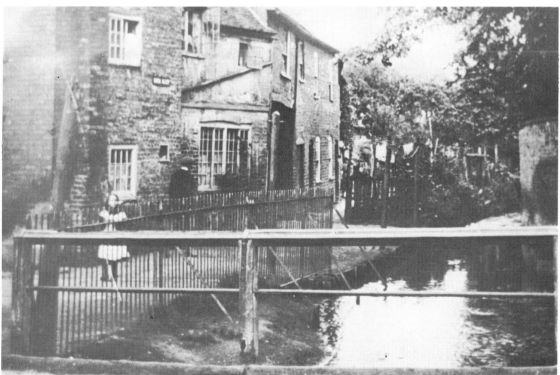

ABOVE: The possible site of Germain street School and
BELOW: Duck Alley, now Page and Thomas' truck access.

ABOVE: The Town Bridge and BELOW: Hard by, looking
across the site of Water meadow car park. (FFC).
RIGHT: King Street.

*ABOVE: The Grove at The Bury and BELOW: the town's
exit to Missenden, with RIGHT: the aftermath of the 1917
flood at Pednor Mead. (FW)*

ABOVE: The Church street/Wey lane cross roads hasn't changed much, though BELOW: The Bury stood prouder in the past, near the site of the Town's Saxon settlement.

ABOVE: As Church street curves towards Market Square, it mourns most of these homes, while once BELOW: The Market Hall arches were open for business, at Chesham's later centre.

ABOVE LEFT: Everyc
town's Church street/H
way traffic was nothing
gathered outside Cox
permitted opposite to
S

24

for the camera at the
:is while RIGHT: one
:LOW LEFT: a crowd
:HT: deliveries were
:ENTRE: the site of

ABOVE: Young's (today's Gutteridge's) and the doctor's house marked the entry to BELOW: Broadway before Brandon's, Station road and the multiple obstructions of the town's original green.

26

The changing face of Broadway seen from High street.

27

*ABOVE: A rare record of the mouth of Blucher street before
Broadway Baptist Church was built and BELOW: after.
INSET: Courses for horses in Broadway.*

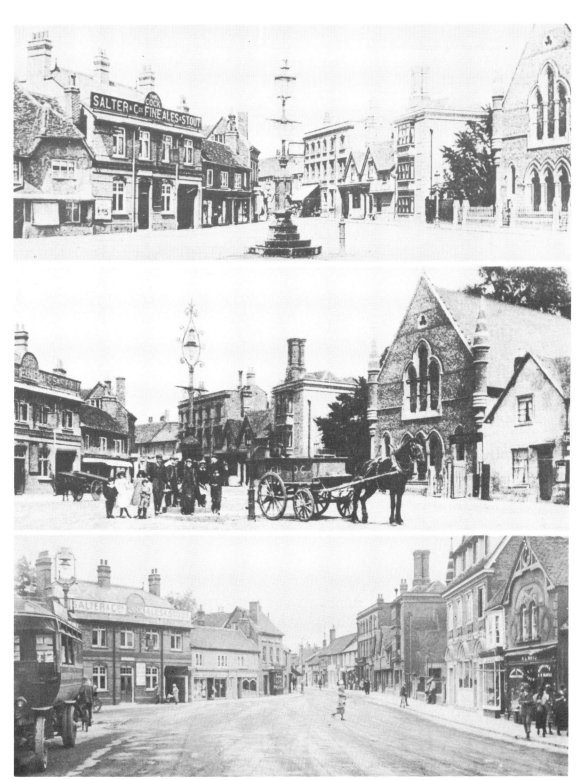

Three lamps in the Broadway mark three changes in the skyline.

*ABOVE: Broadway before Station road; CENTRE: after-
wards but still with Hardings, and BELOW: with the new
cinema. INSET: The sign once on the corner of the
Temperance Hotel.*

30

ABOVE: The rural park at the Church end; CENTRE:
Skottowe's Pond put to good use and BELOW: Park road
leads away towards Chartridge past Catling's Farm (right),
now no more.

31

The one-time pride of Chesham and its Park – Bury Hill Walk.

32

ABOVE: Once Chartridge lane, CENTRE: developing Lowndes avenue between the wars, and BELOW: unilateral housing climbed Hivings hill.

ABOVE: The view from 'The Rec' at Nashleigh Hill and BELOW: across Higham mead, with LEFT: Brockhurst road and RIGHT: the Broad street junction with Eskdale avenue, long ago.

ABOVE: Peaceful Broad street after the departure of
BELOW: Coughtrey's Cottages, once the Pest House.

35

ABOVE: Time to sit and think in Broad street and
BELOW: to take a breather on White Hill.

36

ABOVE: The town from the Church tower and BELOW: from the Station. c. 1900.

ABOVE: Ley Hill, with the old Crown and common right grazing; BELOW: Tylers Hill and RIGHT: Granny Dell, c. 1918. (CC)

THE CENTURY GIVES WAY

What was it like in and around Chesham as the century turned? Employment was scarce for one thing: locals went to help with the potato harvest in the Scilly Isles. Gypsies still camped on the verges, but in those days they had horses and caravans, chickens and dogs — not cars and rusting junk. Wild daffodills grew in the hedgerow, beside the road, and a makeshift farm dinner would include mashed potato, gammon rashers and eggs, followed by fruit pudding.

Granfer Dell died in 1909, and Miss Ford made Granny's widow's bonnets each year, buying a new white frill from Tree's (where Waitrose is now) for 3¾d and washing the black and white ribbons. Born at Woodrow, Amersham, Mr Dell married a Lye Green girl, at St. Mary's, Chesham, and farmed at Hog lane, Ashley Green, later Chartridge, and then Pednor Vale. Every fourth Sunday saw a children's service at Ashley Green church so the children would walk to meet their Granny as far as the chalk dell. The Vicar, the Rev. S.E. Boultbee would enquire when farmer Dell was having the thrashing done, so he could cycle along with his two white Scottie dogs for a day's rat catching!

Church and farm, village and squire all touched each other's lives in a much closer manner than anything we in our classless society can imagine today. For instance, Col. and Lady Smith-Dorrien owned Haresfoot, the strange single storey Georgian mini-mansion that used to stand back from the Berkhamsted road beyond Ashley Green. Theirs was a large family.

One daughter, Miss Beatrice held the Bible Class at St. John's Ashley Green. After morning service, and a picnic lunch, shared in Miss Beatrice's case with the village girls. Miss Maryan dressed the choir — the boys had dark suits, the girls red riding hoods and cloaks, and in summertime a floral print dress, print cape and large leghorn hat with muslin 'rushing' round the crown.

Contrast the drifting elegance of the Sunday rituals with the slog of taking your horse to be shod at Wheeler King's of Ley Hill, from Hog lane, Ashley Green.

Perhaps the best way to imagine Chesham in the first decade of the century is to take a walk on a Sunday morning, with Sidney and Doris Tomlin, Rosie, Caroline and Bertie Climpson, Dorothy and Willie Lewis and George and Connie Lambert.

The walk starts at Fred Channer's Broadway dairy in the town centre; opposite were, among others, Hawes the tailor, the butcher's shop, the Carlton Press, the Lamb, R. Brown's ironmongery, Walter East the newsagent, the Goss tea rooms and Holbeche, Pain and Anderson, estate agents, whose premises were marked outside by a large puddingstone like those in St. Mary's foundations, and those others which once punctuated the road to Hemel Hempstead.

Down the High street, the shop blinds were drawn of a Sunday, and where Waitrose is today there stood Tree's and the doctor's house — Dr. Jno. F. Churchill's, with its neat garden in front and a mature clematis climbing the side wall. As you passed Wm. Young & son (once the late H.M. King and now Gutteridge's) Mr William Young might be glimpsed in his black frock coat, pausing by his parrot, that infallible shopkeeper who, whenever a customer appeared would call 'Shop Mr Young. Shop Mr Young.'

Further along was Wm. Butts, photographer, so many of whose pictures grace these pages, Hobbs the confectioners, pharmacist Abbott and May the jeweller. Wright's tobacconists survives; Lum's Yard, then Darvell's bakery and Wilcock's the tailor preceded the doctors' surgeries, hard by H. Webb's antique shop and Wm. George's premises. Mr. George was a

stalwart of the town, a Union (workhouse) boy who rose to himself become a Guardian of Amersham Union and trustee and executor of many a local estate. Hatter and clothier James Howard was near F. W. Clare's drapery and across the street lay the Crown, proprietor the redoubtable Humphrey Blower.

Mr Piggin always had figs for Palm Sunday in his bow window, but H. Wallace, ironmongers (now Pearce's) had shuttered windows. The corner where the fabric shop stands today was even then Wheeler's drapery.

In the Market square butcher W. Gomme and pork butcher Shadwell led to E. Wright's round the corner, corn chandlers, still with us and until earlier this year run by Wrights.

Where the cinema now stands in Germain street then stood a large and gracious house with shuttered windows behind which were decorously displayed maidenhair ferns. This was the home of Miss Faithorn, who for over fifty years held local bible classes, Miss Ann Potter, her faithful friend and maid. When she died all her Bible class 'lads' who attended the funeral were invited to choose a book each from her library.

Next door was John Gooding's smithy, and opposite, Walter Stratford, undertaker. The old town bridge and King's Arms were not far from the little Sunday School kept by Master William Smith of Wey lane, who was ordinarily clerk to Francis and How, solicitors to the town. In Mr Smith's Sunday School there was an iron stove with a rail round it; the girls sat on forms in the front, and the boys on forms at the side.

Back up the High street, at the junction with Station road, Lloyds Bank was already established, and on that side too lay baker E. Sells, Thos. Carr the silk mercer, his name displayed on his lowered blinds, Swift the jeweller whose small shop discreetly displayed a brass plate, milliner E. G. Ford, W. Clay the butcher, Wm. Thomas the tailor who had a dentist upstairs, and Charles Watts, whose grocery shop was probably Tudor in origin. On the same side were James Herbert's private house, grocer Goodey, the Tap public house, Pandora Stores, H. Cox, harness maker, Reg Baker's cycles, Chilton, the local (Butcher's) bank, Pattersons, Samuel Bunker, hairdresser Bendall and Thomas: fashion store.

Beyond the Crown was a tobacconist, Lewis' fishmongers, grocer Whiteman, and the Market Place centre of Smith Bros., the newsagents (now Chilterns Office Efficiency), Oak Tree Boot and Shoe Store and Sewell's drapery.

On the edge of the town, opposite Amy Mill, only recently sadly demolished, the first house in New road – Orchard House – belonged to milliner Ford – Elizabeth Garrett Ford, with Ann, daughter of William Ford, registrar. The house was then in Chesham Bois parish. Ann became registrar on her father's death and left a bequest to the lad with the best handwriting at Germain street school.

Walks over, there was always Sunday School, and at the church rooms, there was strong competition for the Philip Lord Wharton Bible and Prayer Book. Miss Mildred Wheeler took the recitals of psalms and catechism and one Sunday afternoon, Mrs Sidney Harman of Little Grove Priory sent down crates of jaffa oranges, and the children filed forward for their share. An eye witness records: 'One boy did the unforgivable – he peeled his orange and threw the peel in the gutter instead of taking it home. How clean the streets of Chesham were then.'

IN THE PUBLIC EYE

Chesham's premier public building, the Market Hall,
post war victim of progress.

ABOVE: Laying the main drains in the 1880s BELOW:
drilling for the water supply and   LEFT: the power
station in Higham Road.

*The Fire Brigade, ABOVE: with an early machine, and
BELOW: after 1894.*

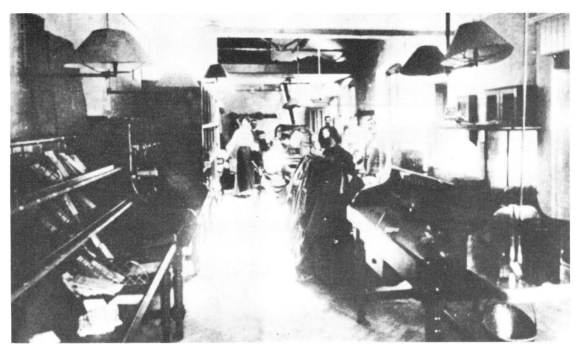

ABOVE: Inside the Post Office in Broadway in Edwardian times, and BELOW: the old Police Station once further along Broad street.

ABOVE: Fund raisers for the Cottage Hospital in the post office yard with BELOW: the Hospital and LEFT: Dr. Jno. F. Churchill.

45

Townsend Group Infants ABOVE: c.1900 and BELOW: in 1913. (FW)

46

ABOVE: White Hill School staff between the wars, (RH)
and BELOW: pageantry earlier this century from the
Foresters' Friendly Society, by Barnes' Boot Factory in
Post Office Yard.

*Sporting gentlemen gathered ABOVE: somewhere near
Chesham last century and BELOW: in the Market square,
earlier in this one.*

48

ABOVE: The relaxing business of local cricket, LEFT: the important Annual Fete Committee of Cricket and Football Clubs in the early 1900s (WR) and RIGHT: a bit of fun which would be frowned upon today, at a venue that doesn't exist today. The Rink was opposite Zion Chapel in Red Lion street.

ABOVE: Cestreham Sports in 1919 (FW) and BELOW: Chesham Generals Reserves, winners of the Aylesbury & District League Cup (1897-8) – the first football cup brought back to Chesham. L. - r. (back): H. Lacey, A. H. Reynolds (Sec), W. Woodley, C. Humphrey, R. Stephenson, G. Webb (Asst. Sec); (middle): F. Stone, W. Dwight, W. Lacey (Capt), W. Dwight; C. Barnes; (bottom): J. Davis, F. Dwight, A. Stephenson. (AJS).

*ABOVE: Chesham Generals shortly before World War I,
at the Football Meadow— in Bellingdon Road, and
BELOW: Chesham United FC 1921-22. (FW)*

War came to Chesham when ABOVE: these Boer War volunteers marched through to battle. CENTRE: This triumphal arch welcomed the town's VC, Henry Hodgkinson home from South Africa and BELOW: this railway across the Moor was not a new rail link, but practice for World War I engineers.

ABOVE: B. Coy., 1st.Btn., Royal Irish Regt., stationed
Agra, India, at Rawal Pindi in 1910 for the hot season,
8761 Pte.Joseph Climpson smoking a pipe directly above
'Haldane's Pet' placard. Under Gen.Sir Horace Smith-Dorrien
of Haresfoot, a gallant stand at Mons, October 1914, left
everyone here wounded or killed. Pte.Climpson never came
back. BELOW: Horse sale at the outbreak of the '14-18
hostilities, August 16, in the Broadway.

*ABOVE: Our lads on parade, 1918, in the Broadway and
BELOW: part of the Peace Day Carnival celebrations in
1919. (FW)*

ABOVE: Planting the Victory Oak in the Park on Peace Day with Frith Lowndes left of the tender plant, and BELOW: Tug Wilson on the Astoria's roof, (then Palace, now Co-op furniture store) filming the unveiling of the War Memorial in the Broadway, 1921.

*ABOVE: Chesham Male Voice Choir, c.1910, conductor
Arthur Gammon (second row, centre), and BELOW: six of
our masters on April 4, 1910 – after the Urban District
Council elections. (Both MH)*

PRIVATE MEANS AND PUBLIC WAYS

In 1820 Chesham was all set to become the Spa of the Chilterns, with the "Chesham Chalybeate". "At a Public Meeting of the Inhabitants of the Town and Parish of Chesham held pursuant to the Public Notice at the Town Hall in Chesham on Monday the 25 Day of Oct in the year 1820 to take into considn the means to be adopted for rendering the Chalybeate Sprg laterly discovered on Chesham Moor beneficial to the Parish . . . " it was agreed that "the land out of which the Mineral Spring issues and the Waste Land adjoining shall be immediately enclosed".

Next the meeting agreed "That for the purpose of preventing any nuisance being committed or any Injury done to the Spring as well as for the convenience of those who may wish to drink the Waters a Building covering the Spring shall at the least possible expence be erected immediately . . ."

The cash for this grandiose scheme was to come from public subscription, and a committee of subscribers chosen to implement the resolutions and regulate their use. Mineral House was built, but the spa never came to much.

Of quite a different nature was the determination of the town's leading citizens to instruct and educate the poor of the parish. On June 29, 1870 a Memorial was addressed to the Trustees of the Chesham Almshouses by the promoters of a scheme to erect a British School. (The original was founded in 1828).

"Your Memorialists haveing heard that you are in possession of a surplus sum of money, which they understand there is some difficulty in applying to the purposes probably most desired by yourselves . . . would earnestly request (etc., etc) . . . "

To drive home their point, the promoters went on "This scheme has the recommendation of being one in which both Churchmen and Nonconformists conjointly and earnestly act . . . for the benefit of the whole Parish. Many efforts of narrower interest might arise . ."

Then came the clincher: "Your Memorialists would beg to call attention to that clause of the enclosed address, in which the financial statement is set forth, and would respectfully suggest that no movement, as it appears to them, would come so near to the purposes aimed at by the Founder of the Charity as that sought by your Memorialists — namely the Education of the Poor."

The Weedon Trustees could not legally comply with this appeal, but the school was built.

In the 1880s when the town borrowed £17,502 at 3¾% over 30 years to pay for drainage and water supply, £50 would buy you a horse, a mare and a cart, while you might pay 13 shillings a day to a ploughman, 2s 6d to a boy and under two pounds a year Poor Rate.

Two decades earlier Winter Fare in January, 1868, was reported thus: 'The poor of Chesham are now supplied with soup every Tuesday and Friday, at the usual place, at 1d. per quart.'

Property was beyond the reach of the ordinary man. The Widow Bennett paid £6 a year for a two down-two up 'Brick built and Tiled Dwelling House', with a large attic, garden, woodhouse and other outbuildings 'well supplied with Water' and found herself with a new landlord in 1813 — he paid £112 for the freehold. Down Waterside, John Gates paid £5 4s for his four roomed cottage with its large garden, productive fruit trees and grazing rights over the Moor, enjoying 'picturesque scenery'. His house changed hands for £74.

Meadowland was worth a penny or two; in 1816 a freehold meadow of something over an acre with '12 choice Fruit Trees' and a timber yard, occupied by J. Fuller Esq., at the west

entrance to the town, sold for £140. The next door cottage, with its five rooms, garden, barn and 'use of a good Well of Water' inclusive of sitting tenant fetched exactly ten times the annual rent of £8, while Mr Stratton bought the smaller tenement next to that — all three rooms of it, and a garden with fruit trees and the use of the well — for £62, against an annual rent income of only £5. All the tenants had been warned to quit by Michaelmas!

All this was a far cry from the sale that same year of Little White End Farm, with 122 acres 3 roods and 11 perches (including the recently bulldozed Lady Wood), described as 'particularly recommended to the notice of sporting Gentlemen, being situate in a neghbourhood abounding with Game, and within a few miles of the Kennel of the Berkley Hounds.'

'The property is most desirably situate on an agreeable eminence, near LAYHILL COMMON, a short distance from CHESHAM . . . and near to the Mansion of THE HON. LORD G. H. CAVENDISH, at LATIMERS, by whose land it is nearly circumscribed . . .' How fashions change. The 'roomy' farmhouse, three barns, stable, cow and cart houses, other buildings, yard, pastures and 13 closes were all on offer. The woodland was on short lease; the rest of the estate let to Mr White 'a respectable Tenant' for £118 a year, seven years to run.

Mr Wilson in 1813 paid £630 for a freehold estate in the High street, comprising a house and shop, and three cottages 'in yard'. There was a 'full Trade in Linen Drapery, Hosiery, Haberdashery, etc.,' the house had five bedrooms, modern kitchen and washhouse, dining and sitting rooms, an 'excellent Well of Water in Yard' and the tenant was Mrs Simpson. The cottages were occupied by Joseph Childs, the Widow Dodd and James Smith 'at moderate rents'. (About £5 per annum).

In 1815 John Potter, Cabinet-maker died, and his "New and well-made Elegant Furniture, choice Stock in Trade, large quantity of tools and other effects" were sold up by auction — the furniture at the Town Hall (not the Market Hall as we call it) and the Stock of Timber etc on the premises. Examples were 'Twelve capital-seasoned cherry-tree inch boards at per foot,' or 'famous 2-inch oak plank and 4-inch ditto all at'; tools included 'Glue pot and pitch kettle' and 'Capital grind stone and frame'. Today's dealers would savour the 'Handsome well-made cherrytree bureau fitted up with drawers complete' or the 'Capital wainscot oak linen-chest with drawer', while the curio hunter might be intrigued by the 'Cheese-box, camp stool and curious grinding machine' that made up Lot 44. And what are we bid for Lot 45? 'Seventeen well-seasoned walnut-tree gun-stocks'? Not much perhaps for Lot 70: 'Tin dutch oven and copper tea-kettle' or Lot 19: 'Four children's pot-chairs and table ditto'. Finally, two of the last items were listed in uneasy proximity: Lot 72: 'Fowling-piece by Morrell' and Lot 73: 'Clean goose feather-bed'. Regrettably, our surviving catalogue is unpriced. Imagine today's values.

Property prices had moved on only a little by 1910, considering a century had all but elapsed. 'Chesham — Charming detached house, in a salubrious position, about 600ft above sea level; 15 minutes' walk from station; exceptionally well built . . . large hall, 2 reception rooms, 3 bedrooms, bathroom (h & c), with lavatory basin and WC, coal-house, shed etc; matured garden. Price £650.' Rents were somewhat higher. 'Commodious semi-detached house, 2 miles from station with hall, 2 reception, 6 bedrooms, bathroom, kitchen and small garden. Rent £28.' On the business side, Hawridge corn mill was to let with house, stabling, sheds, piggeries and garden for £40.

In 1910 population was 8,061 — an increase of 83; 95 deaths or 11.7 and 178 births, or 22.08 Five were illegitimate. Of the 95 deaths, 21 were infants under one year of age, an infant mortality rate of 117.9. Outworkers numbered 261. Two people died of diphtheria,

and there were three cases of scarlet fever. 1,375 ft of sewers were laid. With few exceptions, houses in the district drew water from the public supply. There were six elementary public schools, and 223 nuisances abated. The figures come from the Medical Officer of Health's annual report, in which he commented that visits to dairies during haymaking left him unhappy with the state of their cleanliness, and he had asked one milk carrier not to keep his cans in the living room. He also applauded a county isolation hospital, commenting of the town's building in The Vale 'if you gentlemen were to see the poor children who are confined to one room for six weeks on end, or the poor mother who has charge of them, you would agree with me.'

Nevertheless, there were those who made money. Two Popes, father and son, died in 1801 and 1828. Both were farmers at White End. Their estates were proved at something under £5000 and £4000 respectively, while miller William Puddephatt reckoned his nett value in 1885, including stock and debtors at £2679.5s.

Rather grumpily, the Editor of the *Examiner* in the first 1889 issue observed that things were not what they used to be; one 'would hardly know a (Cherry) fair was being held at all.' The sheep and cattle were scant, and in the Broadway there was only one stall — a 'roll, bowl and pitch' man, with three more in the Market place.

The December 1892 meeting of the Board of Guardians heard that 274 vagrants were processed in a fortnight; in one week the "outside poor" numbered 696. Poor relief cost £78.1s.6d for the quarter. Reported the Poor Law Inspector, Murray Browne of the Workhouse: ". . . venture to urge that both the two wells should be analysed to see whether the water might not be polluted . . . " and " . . . wards which were only lighted with rushlights were surely like darkness visible."

For the working man, it was different. William Birch of Chesham, 'a minor of the age of seventeen years or thereabouts' with his aunt Leticia Birch's consent, became apprenticed to Chesham Builders and Decorators Ltd on January 1, 1920. He was put to the 'Art trade or business of Carpenter and Joiner' for four years, against which his 'Masters . . . shall teach' and find 'the tools necessary for his use' and pay his weekly wage of £1 for the first year, £1.5s the second, £1.12s the third and £2 during the last year 'or the Trade Union Rates for apprentices prevailing in the District'.

And his tools were not cheap; a list tells us something about the craft of woodworking in Chesham at the time: mortice gauge 14s; skew rabbit 11s; spoke shave 2s 6d; pincers 2s 6d; spirit level 2s 6d; (not forgetting the weekly wage was only £1); hammer 7s; plugging chisel 2s 6d; hand saw £1.1s; trying plane £1.5s; jack £1.1s; brace £1.1s; 4 bits 12s 9d; rimer 9d; 12-square 8s; basket 7s 9d; 9" bevel 7s 6d; panel saw 16s 6d; oil slip 1s 10d; 3 carpenter pencils 6d. Altogether 34 items are listed, total cost: £12.0s.0d or in 1920, wages for a lad for some three months. Times have changed indeed.

In April 1920 there were sixteen candidates for six seats on Chesham UDC. The poll was considered poor, at 1600, only 200 having voted by 2 o'clock. Ralph Howard topped the poll with 957 votes, and George Robinson, at fifth position with 487, was the only successful Labour candidate.

MANY MANSIONS

Chesham's independence of spirit led, early on, to questions of faith. It was inevitable that in this town, nonconformity would find fertile minds and souls in which to flourish. But the background is obscured by that same independence, which caused splinter groups and dissension among the dissenters. There follows a list, almost certainly incomplete.

Anglican: St. Mary's Parish Church, est.c.10th century; recorded 1220; built 13th century; restored 14th, 15th, 17th, 18th centuries; major restoration 1869. Christ Church, built 1864; Emmanuel, built 1886; St. George's, Tyler's Hill, built 1871; St. John's, Ashley Green, built 1873.

Catholic: St. Columba, built 1960.

Baptist: Chesham Baptists sign the Orthodox Confession, Aylesbury, 1679; origins traceable to 1676. Particular Baptists organise, (origin of Trinity Church) 1701. Particular (later Old or Lower) Baptist Chapel built 1719, enlarged 1797, rebuilt as Hinton Chapel 1897, became Trinity 1968.
Zion Baptists formed from Lower Baptist splinter group 1868; Zion Chapel built 1873.
Townfield High Calvinistic Baptist Chapel built 1820 (the third Baptist Chapel, with Hinton and Zion, on one acre). Townfield move to become Newtown Baptists; built Chapel 1927.
General Baptist Chapel built 1712, rebuilt three times, finally as Broadway Baptist Church, 1902.
Hivings Park Free Church, a Baptist supported foundation, built 1962.
Chartridge Baptist Chapel, a branch of Broadway, founded 1840s, rebuilt 1880s. Leyhill, Whelpley Hill, Chesham Vale, Ashley Green formerly had Chapels.

Methodist: Evangelistic services held at Town Hall, 1892.
United Free Church established 1907, meeting Town Hall, then Bellingdon road.
Wesleyan Chapel established by 1900, off Broad street (police car park).
United Free Church and Wesleyan Chapel come together at Bellingdon road in the 1930s. Methodist church rebuilt 1965.
Primitive Methodist Chapel built Ley Hill 1887.

United Reformed: Independent Chapel built Broadway 1724; rebuilt as Congregational Church, 1886; now United Reformed Church, with branches at Asheridge and Friendship Hall, Pond Park.

Others: Gospel Hall, Station road, founded 1876, rebuilt 1965.
Elim Tabernacle shared hall, then used Council Chamber, Broadway; part of Pentecostal Movement, which has succeeded them, meeting at St. John's Hall, Victoria road.   Society of Friends: Meeting House rebuilt 1799.
'Tin' tabernacle, built 1889 Bois Moor road, daughter establishment of St. Leonard's Parish Church, Chesham Bois.   Salvation Army Citadel, built 1898.
Seventh Day Adventists — no information, but known to have worshipped in Chesham. Jehovah's Witnesses, Kingdom Hall, off Berkhamsted road, est. post-World War II. Christadelphians, until recently meeting at Progress Hall.
Christian Spiritualist Church, Higham road. The Church of Jesus Christ of Latter Day Saints, recently established in Chesham, at Progress Hall.
Jewish Congregation during World War II; Moslem Congregation now formed.

St. Mary's Church ABOVE: before the 1869 Scott restoration and BELOW: inside when the decor was somewhat different, c. 1880. (FFC)

61

*ABOVE: The ladies of St. Mary's, Chesham around the
church door and the turn of the century; LEFT: inside the
Lower Baptist Chapel (later Hinton) and RIGHT:
announcing events in the new chapel, 1898.*

*Ministers at Hinton: I. W. Payne (1834-1865); 2. J. Cave
(1866-1873); 3. T. Henson (1873-1874); 4. R. Rogers (1876-
1880); 5. T. Armstrong (1881-1889); 6. L. G. Carter
(1890-1905).*

63

Ministers at Zion: 1. A.G.Free (1867-1975); 2. C.Ingram (1875-1877); 3. Ralph Stone (1878-1885); 4. Wm. Holland (1885-1886); 5. R.Hughes (1886-1888); 6. H.Trueman (1890-1896).

64

ABOVE: Zion Baptists earlier this century; BELOW: The old Baptist 'Star Yard' Chapel and INSET: the original Zion Chapel and George Keen, Superintendent of the Sunday School and Chesham's undertaker, c.1900.

*ABOVE: Inside the original General Baptist Chapel in the
Broadway and BELOW: the Independent Chapel, now
United Reformed Church, with INSET: Mr Freeman,
General Baptist organist.*

66

ABOVE: The United Free Church Sunday School parades in Sunnyside and BELOW: St. Mary's Parish Church Sunday and National School with the town's Silver Band in the High street.

ABOVE: An unidentified Chesham church's Sunday School entertainment in the 1920's and BELOW: The original Methodist Church in Bellingdon road.

THE MARVELLOUS RESTORATION TO HEALTH OF MISS ANNIE FREEMAN

'On May 12, 1910, the day of the proclamation in Chesham of His Majesty King George V, Miss Annie Freeman, known as the subject of the 'Chesham Miracle' paid a visit to the Wesleyan Chapel and gave an account of her marvellous restoration to health'. Thus the *Bucks Examiner* reported on May 19 of that year. The chapel was full, and the service reported as 'of a most powerful and impressive character'. Pastor R. Goodrich asked the congregation 'to receive that (sic) message with an open and devout mind, and to give the matter earnest consideration'. Mr Staniford of Hawridge witnessed to both the sickness and the cure, and averred 'the cure had been wrought by the power of God and the strength of Miss Freeman's faith, but it did not follow therefore that every sick person could be cured in the same way.' After the hymn 'God moves in a mysterious way', Miss Freeman, 'amidst a tense stillness, told her powerfully affecting story, a plain unvarnished recital, that appealed to mind and heart with irresistible force, and bore the stamp of sincerity and truth.'

'For twenty-two years she had been a helpless invalid, paralyzed from the waist downward. She had been entirely unable to leave her bed except by being lifted from it, and her feet lay quite flat with no power or feeling, and quite unable to be put to the ground. The entire lower part of the body was in the same state of insensibility.'

Then: 'A twelve-month ago, she had a vision in which she saw distinctly a certain room quite unfamiliar to her, but the room and its furniture were vividly impressed upon her memory, even to a text hanging on the wall "Thou wilt undertake for me". She was left with the firm assurance that she would be cured in that room, wherever it was'. A lengthy passage of scripture was impressed upon her.

'Miss Freeman then simply, and yet dramatically, related how the invitation came to visit a friend at Bellingdon, and though she had not left her room for eighteen years, now she felt impelled to accept. A closed motor car was obtained . . . and the journey was performed almost in a state of stupor owing to the unaccustomed strain . . . On being taken into her friend's drawing room, she recognised it instantly as the room . . . in her vision, even to the text on the wall. This in spite of the fact that the house had not been taken by her friend at the time of the dream, nor did he know of her dream. In response to her earnest request a bed was made up for her in this room, and her faith was so strong that she had outdoor clothing prepared even to her boots. The first sensation of returning life in her lower limbs was a slight tingling in the middle toe of the right foot, until at last the tingling was felt in all the toes. Then one morning she declared positively she heard a distinct voice, "Daughter, I say unto thee arise." She rose, put on a dressing gown and walked to the breakfast room and knocked, saying "May I come in?" Since then she has been constantly walking to and from Hawridge and other places, and none seeing her would think she has been an almost life-long invalid.'

Miss Freeman was reported as preparing to issue her life story complete as a book with before and after photographs. If she did not, then the Bucks Examiner is her memorial and testimony to her miracle.

HERE ARE THE FOOTBALL RESULTS

Chesham Town Football Club played ten home and eight away matches in the 1900-01 season between September 1 and November 24. They won three, lost ten and drew two matches. Chesham Generals were the victors that year in the local derby — the English Cup — but only after a replay. These are the full results for that period.

1900

Sept	1	Sheppey United	H 3-2 win	Oct	13	Brentford	H 0-3
	3	Watford	H 0-3 lost		?	Generals (replay)	H 0-3
	8	Fulham Res.	H 4-2 (!)		20	Wycombe	A 1-3
	10	Tottenham	H 1-1		27	Maidstone	A 0-1
	22	West Norwood	A 4-5	Nov	3	Millwall	A 0-4
	29	Woolwich Arsenal	H 0-3		10	Tottenham Res.	A 0-6
Oct	6	Chesham Generals			17	Fulham	H 3-1
		(1st round, English Cup)			24	Southall	A 0-8 (Ugh)
			A 1-1				

Cricket on the Green, 1910:—   LEY HILL v. SOCIAL CLUB.

'Chesham Town Social Club established a record for the club on Saturday by winning at Ley Hill and they won by a handsome margin, too, as the scores below indicate. Glasgow's very fine bowling was responsible mostly for the cheap dismissal of Ley Hill, and an average of two per wicket for seven wickets was indeed good. The Social Club lost four wickets for 19 runs, and the game was then in a very open state, but J. Moulder and Richardson pulled it round with good scores. In a second innings Ley Hill scored 31 for the loss of four wickets, A. Joiner making 15 not out, and Taylor took three wickets for 12 runs. A note-worthy point is that in the Ley Hill first innings Glasgow took the first six wickets himself, and Puddephatt and E. Joiner were the only ones that could stand against him. Scores:

LEY HILL		SOCIAL CLUB	
H. Smith, c Richardson, b Glasgow	3	S. Taylor, c West, b Fenn	5
G. Puddephatt, b Glasgow	11	J. Mead, c How, b Fenn	1
B. Fenn, b Glasgow	6	A. Moulder, b Fenn	1
E. Joiner, b Glasgow	14	A. Moreton, b Fenn	6
A. Joiner, b Glasgow	0	T. Higgs, b A. Joiner	7
H. Gillett, b Glasgow	1	A. Glasgow, c A. Joiner, b Fenn	5
B. Waller, run out	0	J. Moulder, hit wicket, b E. Jointer	11
W. West, b Moreton	1	W. Richardson, c Puddephatt, b E. Joiner	16
B. Brown, b Moreton	0	A. E. Hall, c How, b E. Joiner	5
W. Plested, b Glasgow	0	S. Massey, c Fenn, b E. Joiner	0
C. How, not out	1	T. Warner, not out	1
Extras	2	Extras	11
Total	39	Total	69

SOCIAL CLUB BOWLING

	O	M	R	W	Avg.
A. Glasgow	7	0	16	7	2.2
W. Richardson	3	0	17	0	0
A. Moreton	3	1	4	2	2

SMALL MATTER

This scurrilous letter was addressed to the Reverend James Sleap of Hinton; (1772-1811) by an anonymous writer. It is undated, but has been preserved with other papers in the files of a Chesham lawyer. It reads:

This his to give Notys that theer his now Lifing hin this towne thee great Hore of Babyllon hand thee Dr. C hav Brodher hof Chanys who by their insinuations hafe taken the Vantage of poor hold punchback to Draw him hin to Mack ha Will hand leave them Hall his hestates hof Nevery kind to the Great hurt hof poor pryses Family

They Mighter hope this would be

Glad hif parson Sleep Will hinform they publict hif his Docturn Can Countenance such Wickedness hin his heart hand himself Wicked Docturn hindeed.

from
J

'Bury Hill Walk, December 1845. The remainder of the Elm Trees, forming the Avenue, (in the Park) were taken down by direction of William Lowndes Esq., the Proprietor, and young Trees planted in their stead. They are supposed to have been planted . . . about 130 years back. During a hurricane in November, 1836, several of the largest . . . were blown down . . . Since then, others have shared the same fate, until at length the entire Grove has disappeared.' And did again in our time, but this time no friendly Squire picked up the tab for a replacement, more's the pity.

'THE FIRE ENGINES Are kept at the Engine House in Amy Lane, of which G. Aris and G. Leaper have each a key. Mr. Collier has the charge of keeping the Engines in repair. The number of Firemen when complete, is 14, but there are at present only 8.' (1845) Chesham's Fire Brigade was formed the following year, with two engines and eighteen firemen.

In February 1846 G.O. Pater 'Returns his grateful thanks to his Friends and the Public in general, for the liberal support they have hitherto given him, and begs to inform that, in consequence of ill health, he has disposed of his Business to Mr James Clare, Junr., and respectfully solicits the continuance of their kind favours to him, feeling convinced that no exertion will be wanting on his part, to merit the same.' They were gentlemen in those days.

'Friday July 17, 1846. Fire occurred by accident at half-past eleven at night, on the premises occupied by Mr N. Reynolds, at Prospect Terrace. Got under by exertions of newly-formed Fire Brigade, aided by inhabitants of the Neighbourhood, including many Females.'

'A petty Session held this day . . . Mr. T. Thomas, of Berkhamstead, a Reporter for several Newspapers, admitted for the purpose of reporting the Proceedings; being the first instance of any Reporter being allowed to be present on these occasions.' January 13, 1847.

'A Vestry held to Nominate Constables etc., at which the Chairman, John Humphries, signed with an X, being unable to write; no other person consenting to take the Chair.' February 17, 1847.

In 1867 James Higgs of Chartridge was fined and bound over for his 'pugnacious pro-clivities' in beating his wife up after drinking at the Porto Bello Arms. When his wife asked him to go home in February 1868, he beat her up again; she took out a warrant, he appeared at the magistrates' Clerk's office and they sent him to prison for six weeks with hard labour.

'William Warner, beerhouse-keeper, was brought up under a warrant' (January 22, 1868) for 'threatening to kill his wife, Sarah'. 'Her husband . . . repeatedly threatened to cut her throat. She was afraid he would do so.' Bound over to keep the peace; 16s 2d costs.

'FOREIGN WINES. GOOD OLD PORT . . . 10s 9d. per Gallon . . . Drawn from the Wood. Try a Sample. DAVID SMITH, READY MONEY TEA SHOP, BROADWAY, CHESHAM.' January 1868.

'STEALING TURNIPS. Edward Birch, labourer, of Chesham, was charged with stealing . . . turnips, value 4d., on Sunday morning' (February 2, 1868). 14 days' imprisonment, with hard labour.

DEATH FROM LOCKJAW. On October 26, 1877 an inquest at the Crown heard how Joseph Atkins, labourer of Hyde Heath met his death. Charles Wright and Atkins worked for B. Fuller of Hyde House, and on October 5, they were 'in the barn threshing lease corn with flails' when, witnessed Wright, 'Joseph's swingle touched mine, and he received a blow from his swingle which slightly wounded him over the right eye, he did not fall down, but went towards the lift to let the blood fall from his head. I said to him "Well Joe I don't know how that happened", he replied "nor I don't know" we then went to the lower part of the barn, and each had a horn of beer; I then put a piece of spider-web on the wound and we went to work again as usual'. 'Dr Churchill saw the victim six days later, and 'found him suffering from . . . lockjaw . . . which resulted in his death.' The jury agreed. *(Note: Swingle — the striking part of a flail: Ed.)*

'The Primitive Methodist preaching place (at Ley Hill) was crowded to excess' (January 22, 1887) for a lecture 'which drew together members of Church and Dissent'. The lecturer 'spoke for an hour and a half without any notes, had perfect mastery over his subject, and everybody present seemed highly delighted . . . a collection was taken in aid of a new chapel for Ley Hill.'

'The cottage homes of Whelpley Hill have this week (January 28, 1887) been gladdened by a seasonable gift of coals, provided by the kindness of Mrs. Constable Curtiss. This is the second gift of the kind from the same generous donor, the first being distributed in time to make bright and warm firesides for Christmas Day.'

In October 1889, there were raised eyebrows and some mirth when the following advertise-ment appeared locally: 'A widower, age 61, wishes to marry again to a lady aged 30-45 of industrious habits. Has ropemaking business. Height 5'8". Complexion fair, eyes grey. I am a composer of music and poetry. One with a small income preferred.' The *Examiner* repeated the advertisement, commenting the advertiser could be found within a hundred miles of Chesham Town Hall. The following week this reply appeared in the *Examiner:*

'Sir, Seeing your advertisement applying for a wife, I thought there would be no harm in meeting you and seeing if we can make any arrangements, as I am in want of a husband. I am 31 years of age, tall, fair and have brown eyes and auburn hair. I am sorry to say my income is not much: I have not more than 12s 6d per week, but hope this will not make any difference. Believe me, I would try and make you a good and loving wife. Will you give me a trial? I shall arrive at Chesham Station tomorrow evening (Thursday) by the 8.40 train.
Will you meet me and oblige,
Yours sincerely,
Kate Morley
PS Not knowing you, can you wear a red geranium for me to recognise you by and I will be wearing three white roses at my throat.'
Between 300 and 400 people turned up for the tryst on the platform next day, but alas, the suitor had been taken to another station, and the lady never turned up. It was all a hoax.

'We are sorry to note that antipathy exists between the two leading football clubs — it is not pleasant for visitors to hear the teams yelled at by their fellow townsmen.' *Advertiser*, October 22, 1892.

'Pig keeping existed at Ley Hill, against the law.' November 1892.

'The Corn Market . . . was something like the weather on Wednesday — very dull — more corn than purchasers.' November 1892.

When two youngsters were fined 2s 6d for playing football 'in the public streets', the police observed 'It is becoming a nuisance in the dinner hour.' December 1892.

Entertainment in January 1903: The Chesham String Band, and the Chesham 'Wee-Wah' All Minstrel Troupe.

Thomas Lee and George King, boothands of Chesham, in court at the Town Hall, April 25, 1903 had been to the fair in the Nag's Head Meadow, when the police saw them 'reeling together, quarrelling and swearing.' They tried to help them home, but the two men were violent and would 'not go home for any b------ police'. Eight weeks, and seven and a half weeks' prison respectively.

'Wanted, all kinds of Maids at once; good wages; good outings; no washing; Maids no fees. 19, High street, Chesham.' 1910.

'Wanted to rent, near Chesham, Small house with three to four acres, suitable for poultry; rent from £18 to £20 per annum, or would purchase on terms. Box 18, Examiner office, Chesham.' 1910.

J. Brandon & Sons offered with every £15 worth of furnishings bought, a free gold wedding ring. 1903.

"Wanted. An intelligent youth (one from school preferred) as an apprentice to the printing trade. Apply H, Offices of this paper." September 1903.

Leonard and Robert Wright faced the Court at Chesham Town Hall (sic) in May 1910, summoned under the Poaching Prevention Act. Leonard pleaded guilty to stealing seven artificial partridge eggs planted by gamekeeper Henry Skinner in a nest in Dry Dell lane on the Lowndes estate. Robert was stopped by Police Sergeant Callaway at Pednor, tried to rush past him, closed with him and fell into the hedge. A five minute struggle ended with the sergeant trying to search Robert, who, 'hit him in the mouth, making his lip bleed. Witness knocked him down and held him on the ground', and there was a struggle for about fifteen minutes. Back at the station, the sergeant was in a state. His lip was bruised and bleeding, his collar partly off, tie disarranged, jacket and trousers dirty. The Super-intendent 'did not think the condition of the sergeant's lip was caused by him falling on the ground.' Robert was fined 20s and costs for assualt, and a further 10s for poaching.

'Who, looking down on thee, and knowing not
Could guess the hive of industry that lies
Beneath these hills? Thy towns both old and new
Joined by thy narrow High-street, isthmus-like —
Shew to the world the crafts thy folk pursue.' (extract from much more in this vein by L.L.B. 1910).

February 1911: Chesham Court. William Sansom was summoned for failing to send his son to school. Mrs Sansom was in court, and said she was guilty — she kept the boy home to 'earn a little bread.' He had missed 59 out of 124 schooldays, for he was kept home to sell newspapers; Mr Sansom was 76 and had five shillings a week pension. The boy was 13. Fined 2s 6d.

Six children, husband and wife, their daughter and baby lived in a three roomed cottage in Inkerman terrace. They were accused of neglecting their children. The court heard how the children were poorly nourished, unclean and verminous. There were 'fleas jumping about on the bed: about a dozen fleas to the square foot.' Husband: case adjourned for 3 months; wife: one month with hard labour.

'Advertiser wishes to meet lady to share sitting room and live with her; terms moderate.' *Examiner*, Jan 16, 1920.

'Why not call on Mrs Batson, 146 Waterside, to see the latest Hats from a London firm for 4s 6d each.?' 1920.

'Good home, with nice people, wanted for baby from few days old, end of April. Box 55.' 1920.

The first season of the Chesham United FC, after the amalgamation of Generals and Town FC 'began gloriously and ended poorly.' The team won the Bucks Charity Cup, and did well in other Cup competitions, but 'the League record speaks for itself — when Chesham was winning Cup matches they could not be playing League matches.' *Examiner*, May 1920.

' . . . the weeds had been cleared from the river . . . suggesting that boating be allowed . . . It was pointed out that the river was not in a condition for boating at present.' *Examiner* report of Chesham UDC meeting, July 1920.

IN THE RIGHT SPIRIT

LEFT: Charles Howard's licence to sell beer, ale, porter, cider and perry at the Rose and Crown, Waterside, in 1858 (MH) with RIGHT and BELOW: E. Wallington's home—brewed ginger beer bottle and mineral water jug. (AS)

An historic Chesham pub crawl might start ABOVE: at the Pack Horse, and BELOW: pass onto the Pheasant, both in Waterside.

76

LEFT: The Five Bells was worth a Waterside pause, and
RIGHT: William Green welcomed you down the road to the
Forester's Tavern, while BELOW: the White Horse was not
far from the early fuel facility on the London road.

ABOVE: Over the Moor at The Unicorn the ladies might take a breather while BELOW: back at The White Horse Mr Whittle and family took a few moments off for the camera.

ABOVE: The Nag's Head in Red Lion street was convenient for the sheep market held in its yard, and BELOW: across the road, the Punch Bowl was fading away to make room for Hinton Chapel in the 1890s.

*LEFT: Up Townfield, the White Lion might best be avoided
as a trouble spot in favour of RIGHT: the cosy Chequers
in Market square or BELOW: the nearby Red Lion, clearly
well supplied by the brewer's drayman.*

ABOVE: The Old King's Arms, King street, gave you a good send-off for an outing, while BELOW: John William Rock kept a bounteous cellar at the Queen's Head round in Church street.

81

Old Houses,
Chesham.

ABOVE: Church street was something of a challenge, among its many hostelries the Star and Garter with the Old Sun Lodging House opposite, and BELOW: the centrally placed and ever-friendly Golden Ball of H.T.Wing. Down the road was the Seven Stars.

*ABOVE: The Crown Hotel and Posting House dominated
the Church street end of High street, and RIGHT: round
the corner in the town's main thoroughfare was the George
and Dragon, Commercial Hotel, run by Humphrey Blower.
BELOW: You might meet Howards (left and
(Phil, the Town Crier) right,) with friends including Chesham's
sweep, 'Uncle' Summerlin, Mr Best the Church street lodging
house keeper and Fred Ringsell, and RIGHT: 'Boomer'
Summerlin (centre) with friends at
the Golden Ball (GS)*

*ABOVE: The High street boasted several 'houses', not least
the Stag, whose landlord doubled as shopkeeper, and LEFT:
in the Broadway was the Johnny-come-lately and unlamented
Lamb, while RIGHT: The Blue Ball offered an off-centre
jar in Blucher street.*

ABOVE: The Plough provided an excuse for gathering strength before climbing White Hill, and BELOW: after that first exhausting few yards, the old Three Tuns stood poised on the first bend.

85

*ABOVE: Decades of refreshing service by the Climpsons
started with the original Waggon and Horses opposite White
hill, and BELOW: good friends gathered for a friendly
darts game then as now, on December 26, 1911, at the
Griffin in Bellingdon road.*

ABOVE: What a welcome was there at the Jolly Sportsman, once INSET: not at the foot of Eskdale avenue, because the road wasn't there then. BELOW: the Nashleigh Arms sped you on your way towards the Vale, and out of town.

*In 1912 Mr Ernest Climpson offered an authoritative
round-up of The Inns of England.*

LICENSED COMMON BREWSTERS

In 1846 Mr J. W. Geary ran the George Inn and Wm. Christmas the Crown Inn: four years prior, the Tithe Commissioners had listed 29 beershops, inns and public houses in the town centre alone. Among them are several forgotten pubs — the Star PH in Blucher street, run by Thomas Stone where now the car park stands; the Green Man, more or less opposite The Limes in High street, licensed to William Archer; on the present site of Litton's, the Royal Oak, in the charge of William Birdseye; the Crown where Tesco stands — a fine Georgian building that should never have come down, punctuating the junction of Church and High street with Market place.

The Punch Bowl Inn stood on the site of today's Hinton Baptist Chapel and Henry Stone officiated; the Nag's Head, just below the Red Lion where now the staff of the Dept. of Employment park their motors played host to the sheep market with Robert Oldfield as tenant. Robert Plested ran the Globe in Market Place, right by the Chequers of William Barnes; strangely it was Plested who ran the bakehouse as well as the pub, since Barnes is a name still associated with bread today. Both pubs were in the run of buildings on the Germain-street/Church street side of the road.

Round in Church street the Seven Stars was occupied by Richard Hearn and Thomas Asprey, and there also was a wheeler's shop; the building has long gone, but was approximately where the cars park opposite the Golden Ball. Thomas Fassnidge jnr. ran the Two Brewers five doors further along Church street, and the Mermaid was opposite the last house on the same side as the Bury, just before you come to the Bury gates. Charles Somes presided.

The Dolphin beershop was almost opposite Weylands, once the grammar school, now a private house, and William Stratford was shopkeeper. The Bell Beershop, often depicted as the Bell Inn where now stands the off licence, was in fact at that time, the first building along Pednor Mead, just behind the present premises. There is clear evidence and belief in the established frontage onto Church street, so this suggests the inn faced onto Pednor Mead rather than Church street, with what would have been its 'back' onto Church street.

Later records and recollections identify often vanished alehouses. One casualty was the Forester's Tavern, so called because the Foresters' friendly Society met there - its location was 98 Waterside. The New Inn, near the railway bridge, Waterside was originally the New Engine, deriving doubtless from its proximity to the railway. Near the new housing development in Waterside, not so long ago the Royal Bucks Laundry, the Elephant and Castle reflects the countrywide interest in the Infanta of Castile.

One name that often crops up on old 'Codd' lemonade bottles unearthed from local Victorian and later rubbish dumps is Wallington. He kept the Rose and Crown down Waterside, and was kinsman to a local High Court judge, Sir Hubert of the same name.

The Five Bells at 282 Waterside once stood in front of the Steam sawmills of Joseph La Verne — he called them his New Prospect Steam Sawmills — and another Mermaid was to be found by Christ Church. Theophilus Plato, scrivener kept a remembered but unnamed public house opposite Lords Mill "by Bass's stile" and not so long ago 'Long Tom' Johnson kept the Spread Eagle, opposite the then coalyard, next to the Pheasant. The Black Horse, Waterside, was originally the Pack Horse, at the foot of Chessmount Rise, and another sporting name graced the Horse and Jockey or Groom once run by Samuel Harris in Germain street — between King street and the new footpath. Was this perhaps the Dolphin

by another name?

Blucher street, itself rapidly disappearing with each road development, was once Bury Hill, and apart from the Star, boasted two other pubs, one the Blue Ball, on the carpark side, the other the Carpenters' Arms. The Old Sun, reputedly once a place of rest for pilgrims, became the Sun Lodging House, and then found itself removed lock, stock and barrel to Pednor in 1938. It's still there, though it used to be in Church street, not far from the Temperance Hall. Its old advertisement ran "Sarah How and Sons, Licensed Common Brewsters.''

In High street the Tap stood where Baxter's is today — it led to Darvell's Brewery. By 1864 the George and the Crown retained their significance, being posting houses for the coach trade, and now joined by the Red Lion. Edward Hancock ran the Porto Bello Arms in Chartridge, now a private house and the Star of Blucher street had become the One Star — perhaps to distinguish it from the Seven? The Star and Garter was by Church Hill — today's antique shop.

In 1864 the Golden Ball was the Excise Office, and a Wallington ran the Hen and Chickens at Botley. By 1888 the Crown was billed as a "Headquarters for cyclists and tourists" and the proprietor of the Golden Ball was no longer in Excise but the meat trade, with a butchery in Market place. Geo. Hepwell Green kept the balance by managing the Chess Vale Temperance Hotel in High street — now Gatsby's, and a toy shop. Here was once the Literary Institute. The Cricketers Inn appeared in High street, proprietor David Wilson, and Alfred Walker took over the Three Tuns, White hill, where the open bend is now, and the family stayed there until 1963, when it was scheduled for demolition, occupied by the Council and eventually pulled down. According to the aggregate of all the records available to date, the beershops, pubs, taverns, inns and hostelries of all kinds in the town total a proveable 75 — over one for approximately every 100 inhabitants, man, woman and child, at the end of the last century. In fact the licensing sessions of September 1889 for Chesham and District threw out one application, and granted 70 others giving 1 licensed house for every 109 members of the population of 7638. Here they are.

Waterside - Black (Pack) Horse, Pheasant, Spread Eagle, unnamed beershop by Bass's stile, Mermaid, Five Bells, Rose and Crown, Elephant and Castle, New Engine (Inn), Foresters' Tavern, five beershops at no's 95, 144, 185, 272 and 422 Waterside; *Bois Moor road* - Unicorn, or Railway Hotel; *London road* - White Horse; *Red Lion street* - Punch Bowl (Prince of Wales), Nag's Head and a beershop at no 30; *Townfield* - White Lion and a beershop at no 41; *King street* - Old King's Arms; *Germain street* - Horse and Jockey/Groom and beershop at no 10; Dolphin (?); *Church street* - Queen's Head, The Old Sun, (Old) Bell beershop, Mermaid, Two Brewers, Star and Garter, Seven Stars, Golden Ball, Cherry Tree, and no's 10, 82 and 109, beershops; *Market square* - Globe, Chequers, Fox and Hounds; *High street* - Crown, George & Dragon, Green Man, Royal Oak, Huntsman, Tap, Stag, Chess Vale Temperance Hotel, Plough, Waggon and Horses, the Vine, and a beershop at 52 High street; *Broadway* - Lamb, Cock; *Blucher street* - Blue Ball, one Star, Carpenters' Arms; *Station road* - beershop at no 30; *White hill* - Three Tuns; *Broad street* - Jolly Sportsman; *Berkhamsted road* - New Inn, Nashleigh Arms; *The Vale* - Black Horse; *Botley street* - Hen and Chickens; *Tylers hill* - Five Bells; *Bellingdon road* - Griffin; *Townsend road* - Archie Moore's beershop at no 35; *George street* - Bateman's beershop at no 47; *Lycrome road* - Black Cat; *Chartridge* - Porto Bello Arms, Bell; *Ley hill* - Swan, Crown; *Asheridge* - Blue Ball.

TO BE

SOLD BY AUCTION,

By J. POTTER,

On THURSDAY and FRIDAY the 18th and 19th
Days of OCTOBER, 1810,

ON THE PREMISES,

At GREAT BROCKAS FARM, in the Parish of CHESHAM;

THE

OUSEHOLD FURNITURE,

LIVE AND DEAD

FARMING STOCK,

And other Effects,

Of Mr. Richard Birch, Deceased;

COMPRISING

Capital Milch Cows; a Fat Calf; capital Nag and Cart Horses;
Store Pigs; Quantity of Wheat in the Rick; Quantity of Oats, and
Barley in ditto; several Ricks of Hay; Market Cart, Ploughs;
Harrows; Barn Tackle; Steel Malt Mill; Feather and Flock Beds;
Blankets and Quilts; Four-post and other Bedsteads; Tables; Chairs;
Glasses, &c. Several Pair of Sheets; Brewing Copper, and Tubs;
Iron-bound Casks; Kitchen Utensils in General; Quantity of Coals and
Wood, and a great variety of useful Articles, which will be particularized
Catalogues, which may be had at the Place of Sale; the Inns in the
Neighbourhood and of the Auctioneer, Chesham, Bucks.

The Sale to begin at Twelve o'Clock each Day.

J. — Marshall, Printer, Aylesbury.

*At Brockas (Brockhurst) Farm, Lye Green road, on October
18, and 19, 1810 Richard Birch's stock and effects were sold
off. (RC) This auction poster was found in Cameo House,
Broadway during restorations this year.*

91

ABOVE: A local unidentified farm typical of the several establishments marking the ridges above the town, and BELOW: a main source of employment and income in the Chesham area. INSET: Our 'famous' Chesham mill, removed to Lacey Green in 1821.

ABOVE: Power house for Chesham's industrial prosperity for centuries were the mills; Lords Mill survives (just) from early Tudor times. BELOW: Farming came close to home, along the Backs.

*ABOVE: The Chess and cress were synoymous for
generations; the cress beds seen from the railway bridge
over Bois road and CENTRE: at Waterside near the railway
bridge. BELOW: The sheep market at the Nag's Head,
natural heir to the chalk hill grazing above the town.*

HEPBURN AND GALE,
LIMITED.

1610

Memorandum of Association.

1. The name of the Company is "HEPBURN & GALE, LIMITED."

2. The Registered Office of the Company will be situate in England.

3. The objects for which the Company is established are :—

   (a) To carry on the business of tanners, curriers, leather merchants, manufacturers of leather belting, hose pipes, and all leather articles for mechanical purposes.

   (b) To buy and sell leather, hides, bark and tanning materials, either as principals or as factors, or agents for others.

   (c) To manufacture and deal in all kinds of leather for boots and shoes, coach harness, upholstery, or other useful or ornamental purposes, or for any purposes of the above trades, and to carry on the business of hide and skin splitting, enamelling and japanning.

LEFT: The 1884 incorporation of Hepburn and Gale Ltd - a reminder of Chesham's great tanning industry of the 19th century, and RIGHT: the surviving cottage where the straw plaiters learnt their craft in Waterside. BELOW: Drawing the timber that underlay the town's eminence in the woodworking trades.

ABOVE: Chesham's timber hauliers stop for lunch, and
BELOW: East's first wood yard in White hill, at Martyr's
Dell.

ABOVE: Thos. Wright's first mill, in Waterside, and BELOW: some of the products. (Both CHD)

97

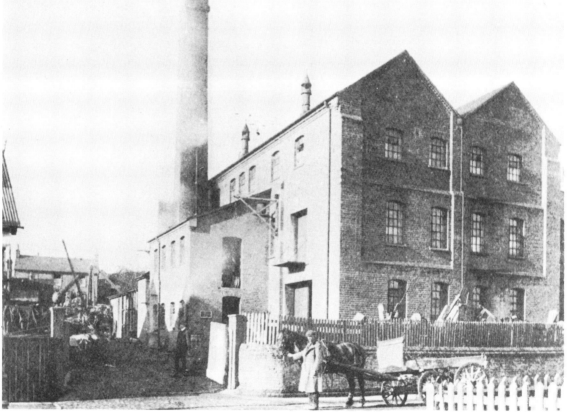

ABOVE: Thos. Wright's second mill, in Berkhamsted road –
before the fire and BELOW: the rebuilt mill. (Both CHD)

*ABOVE: Woodworkers at Webb's Cameron road works,
and BELOW: employees outside the later Wright mill. (CHD)*

ABOVE: The size of this Wey lane consignment of wooden spades from Jesse Wright's works indicates Chesham's skills in selling as well as making woodware, and BELOW: explains the need for massive timbers like this one for Thos. Wright's.

ABOVE: Jesse Wright's yard at Water lane, and CENTRE:
the original Gas and Coke Co. HQ off Waterside, with
BELOW: boiler and engine en route to Beechwood's factory,
c.1911 and in use until 1964/5. (DJN)

101

ABOVE: R.Webb and Sons' employees celebrate Mr and Mrs Geo. Webb's Golden Wedding on May 12, 1914, while CENTRE: Reynolds Boot Factory workers gather for posterity in Blucher street and BELOW: the Carlton Press ladies go on the spree June 22, 1918.

ABOVE: Chesham Brewery, once in White hill where the farmers have their modern cooperative offices, and BELOW: the old silk mill which became the Royal Bucks Laundry, recently demolished for residential development in Gordon road.

ABONE NEWSAGENT & TOBACCONIST STATIONERY

CHRONICLE
TARIFF 'REFORMERS' ON THE RUN

DAILY EXPRESS
MR BALFOUR SAYS 'TRUST THE PEOPLE'

Daily News
MR. ASQUITH ADDRESSES 8,000 MEN ON THE FIGHTING ISSUE

Daily Mail
BALFOUR'S BOLD STROKE

WILLIAM MOORE

W. BUT

Chesham Ph

42, High St., A
CH

PORTRAITS IN ALL
Great Variety of the

Pr

Cabinets from 12
For Painting Cabine
Carte de Visite, fro
Finished in
All other sizes, in
prop
Finest Bromide Enl
Bla
From 10/- in Water

Photographs for Cata
Purposes by Spe
(See G

Children's & Ani

Any and everythi
No Order too

Picture Framin
Testimonials rece

*ABOVE LEFT: Alfre
shop in Berkhamsted r
his dad offered swee
Townsend road, wher
Mr Butts helped m
photographs came f
White's, now Brackle
while BELOW: Wilfred*

ed the papers from his
OW: Archie Moore and
I beer from theirs in
ked bread. CENTRE:
– many of the old
1. ABOVE RIGHT:
et were travel agents
started here at no. 96.

ABOVE: The Co-op brought the shop to the door well into recent years; LEFT: dairyman White moved to what became Chesham Dairies and is now a picture-frame shop in Broad street. Wilfred White, his father and Jack Gomm on the right in 1910. RIGHT: Wilfred (25 in this shot) started in 1903 aged 14, delivering by yoke and pail. (FW).

ABOVE: W.Foster moved to Amersham, and have since departed, but here they occupied the site of Sainsbury's; BELOW: these shops in the High Street were by Stone's timber yard.

At the other end of the High street ABOVE: H. Wallace (now Pearce's) displayed its wares and BELOW: further along in Market Square, H.L.Sewell was well lit from the new gaslamp.

ABOVE: Barclays Bank now occupies this site, CENTRE:
this woodware shop once in the Broadway (next to today's
Chittenden's) later belonged to the Misses Catling, who
BELOW: boasted two emporia, this one in High street.

ABOVE: The House of Tree finally absorbed its neighbour, Dr. Churchill's house, and itself gave way to Waitrose, while BELOW: Abbott's offered greens when the Stag was at bay out of hours.

Darvells made a modest move in High street

111

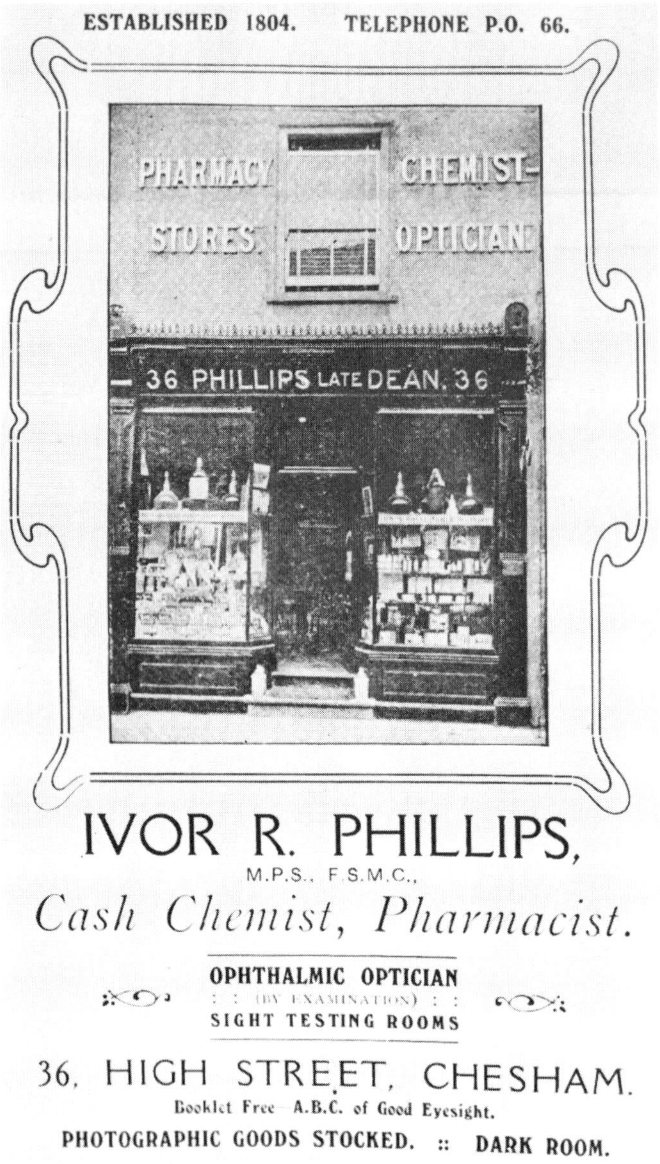
ESTABLISHED 1804. TELEPHONE P.O. 66.
PHARMACY STORES.
CHEMIST- OPTICIAN
36 PHILLIPS LATE DEAN. 36
IVOR R. PHILLIPS,
M.P.S., F.S.M.C.,
Cash Chemist, Pharmacist.
OPHTHALMIC OPTICIAN
: : (BY EXAMINATION) : :
SIGHT TESTING ROOMS
36, HIGH STREET, CHESHAM.
Booklet Free—A.B.C. of Good Eyesight.
PHOTOGRAPHIC GOODS STOCKED. :: DARK ROOM.

F. C. BENDALL,
The County Hairdresser and Tobacconist,
BEGS to thank his numerous customers for the kind support he has received from them during the past ten years, and assures them that they may rely upon receiving the best attention.
FIRST-CLASS ASSISTANTS ONLY ENGAGED.
Bring your Combings.
All kinds of Ornamental Hair Work Executed on the Premises.
Ladies' Haircutting, 6d. ; Singeing, 6d. ; Shampooing and Hair Dried by Electricity, 1s. ; Hairdressing, 1s. ; Dressing and Waving, 1s. 6d.; Manicure, 1s.
Orders by Post receive Prompt Attention.
FAMILIES WAITED ON AT THEIR OWN RESIDENCE IF REQUIRED
CITY AND WEST END EXPERIENCE.
Address : 5 High Street, CHESHAM.

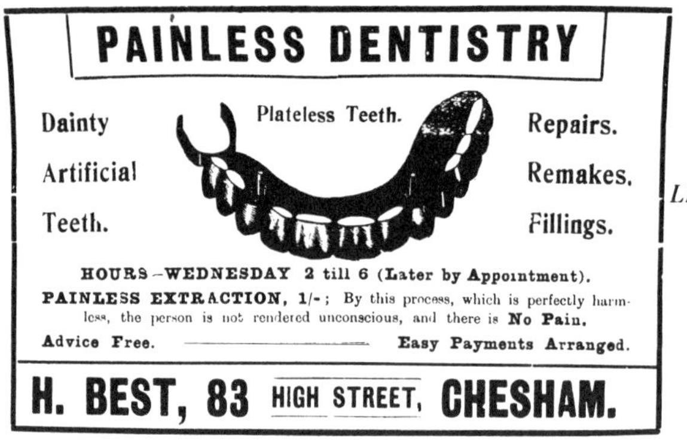
PAINLESS DENTISTRY
Dainty Artificial Teeth.
Plateless Teeth.
Repairs. Remakes. Fillings.
HOURS—WEDNESDAY 2 till 6 (Later by Appointment).
PAINLESS EXTRACTION, 1/- ; By this process, which is perfectly harmless, the person is not rendered unconscious, and there is No Pain.
Advice Free. Easy Payments Arranged.
H. BEST, 83 HIGH STREET, CHESHAM.

LEFT: Phillips has become Garlick's and RIGHT: Mr Bendall offered a wide range of personal services, while BELOW: the dentist was most reassuring.

ABOVE LEFT: The pawnbroker was appropriately near the Golden Ball, and RIGHT: summer heating prices were attractive at Trowers; BELOW LEFT: Wright's has changed little, and RIGHT: Smith's had this Station road outlet as well as their High street shop (now Chilterns Office Efficiency.)

ABOVE LEFT: Almond's famous sweet shop in Red Lion street and RIGHT: the Duck Alley equally famous confectioners opposite the Powell's present one near Town Bridge. BELOW LEFT: Brazil's of Red Lion street and RIGHT: Rose's stores in Waterside, currently closed and for sale, also the post office.

ACCOMMODATING CARRIERS

In the middle of the 19th century, Chesham walked, rode or went by horse drawn coach, carriage or cart. The town's direct link with London in the 1840's was by carrier. Red Lion street in those days was London Road. Thomas Catling left the town at two o'clock on Monday, Wednesday and Friday, taking the Rickmansworth and Watford route. His terminus was the Bell Inn, Warwick lane. He returned the following day, leaving town at one o'clock.

Benjamin Sills left at the same time Mondays and Thursdays, but his route was by way of the Chalfonts and Uxbridge, and his destination the Rose Inn at Smithfield. He also offered a waggon service for calves, sheep and lambs, Thursdays only, leaving the George at 11 am. He arrived at Smithfield Market at 3 am the following morning! His coach customers could return from London Tuesdays and Fridays at two.

George Coughtrey went the Chalfont route also, to the George Inn, Snow Hill on the same days as Mr Sills, but returning from London two hours earlier.

Joseph Climpson offered a twice weekly service Tuesdays and Fridays departing at 2 pm via Rickmansworth and Pinner to the Saracen's Head, Snow Hill, and returning midday the following days.

Other carriers handled local traffic: Robert Oldfield left Chesham at 5.30 Friday, and Saturday at ten for High Wycombe, while William Cheese gave a midday service Wednesdays and Saturdays, putting up at the Crown, Chesham. James Smith connected us with Hemel Hempstead on Thursdays — he made an early start in the summer at 6.30 but left it another hour and a half in the winter. Friday was Tring day for Mr Smith, who offered a Saturday service to Flaunden every other week.

George Hewitt added to Saturday's traffic with a seven o'clock departure for Aylesbury; Samuel Hearn left town for the same destination, fifteen minutes earlier on the same day, while Josiah Hill catered for the late risers at 'a Quarter before Eight' both Saturdays and Wednesdays, and gave an evening service to Amersham 12 hours later.

Samuel Hearn also left for Missenden, Thame and Risborough every Tuesday Morning, from his house, Germain Street, Chesham, at 6 o'clock. Joseph Halt ran from Amersham to Berkhamsted via Chesham and returned the same evening on a Wednesday, while on Thursdays he gave a service to Beaconsfield and Windsor from Amersham. Thomas Slade gave a same day return service to Bovingdon, while John Putnam left Monday and Friday at 1 for Missenden and Tuesday, Thursday and Saturday at 9.30 for Watford.

William Dormer concentrated on goods traffic — to Berkhamsted twice a week and once to Amersham, while Charles Newton handled The Lee and Gt. Missenden freight, and E. Brandon 'carries light Parcels from Chesham to Latimer daily' and the only man at everyone's beck and call was the astute J. Grover, who undertook light parcels delivery: 'J. Grover of Church Street — carries light Parcels to any place required'.

The mails were conveyed by Mr W. Saunders and thence by train. 'The box closes for the London Mail at 10 min. past 7.p.m.' announced Post Master George Devereux. 'Letters posted after that time pay extra 1d each until 20 min. past 7; after which time they are too late for that day's Post.'

Letters for Missenden and Wendover were delivered the next morning; registered letters had to be mailed half an hour before the box closed. And if you wanted your mail before

the postman came your way, why you could call for them personally, but 'the Post Master is entitled to charge for an early delivery'. Office hours for issue of money orders were 9 – 6, and residents were sternly advised that 'The letter carrier is not allowed to deliver a letter to any person in the street'.

But among the more important transport facilities of 1846 was Barnes's Chesham and Rickmansworth Railway Coach, which left the George daily except Sundays for Watford Station. From February to November, it left at '20m bef. 8 . . . punctually'. Arrival time in town was 10.15 am. The coach left Watford in the evenings at 5.30, Chesham-bound.

After November, winter schedules operated. The coach arrived at Watford 'in time for 25 m.pt.9 Up Train' and returned from Watford 'On the arrival of the 10 min.past 4 pm Down Train from London'.

In addition, there were six trains to London daily from Berkhamsted, and seven from London. This nearby facility was extolled by advertising that would sound good to infl-ation-ridden commuters of today: 'Reduced Fares by the London & Birmingham Railway'.

That same year under the heading 'Buckinghamshire Railway' Chesham's *Almanack* recorded the report of Directors, dated August 26, that 'the Line from Oxford to Bletchley, also that from Banbury to Tring, will be proceeded with; but . . . the line from Aylesbury to Harrow, (which was intended to pass between Chesham and Amersham,) will *not* be con-structed.'

The change the railway brought was foreshadowed by this earliest printed reference to local transport in 1845:
'Oct. 6. The Accomodation Chesham Coach, which was commenced by the late W. Wyatt, and had continued to run between this Town and London daily for many years, was dis-continued, owing to the increase of Railway Travelling'. This entry is just followed by one for November 5, which after describing the survey in the Parish for the railway line 'along the top of Town Field by the Beech Tree, by White Hill, *and past Mr Field's house in the Vale*' (my italics - Ed), went on to say 'The Company did not deposit their plans with the Clerk of the Peace by the 30th November, consequently the project cannot be brought before Parliament at the ensuing Session'.

The line to Boxmoor from London had opened in July 1837 and was extended to Tring in October, and this gave Chesham its first taste of the railway age. Although the earlier Grand Junction Canal had attracted Chesham's goods traffic to some extent, it was the railway that rapidly established a connection between the two towns as never before.

The relationship prospered, far transcending anything foisted on Chesham and Amersham in recent times, thus belying man-made administrative bonds. Many permanent links were forged by marriage as a direct result of the cross-flow of people, and when both towns had pawn shops, each would use the other's facility, to avoid nosey neighbours.

The road through the Hockeridges saw the passage of the horse drawn L & NWR rail-way coach, the local carriers' carts, and later, the steam-powered freight waggons carrying at one time £10,000 worth of goods. Such was the Chesham 'presence' in Berkhamsted that when a new (Lower King's) road was planned to the station, Chesham people were asked to stump up their share.

In 1887, two years before the Metropolitan line reached Chesham, there was a scheme to connect Chesham, Boxmoor, Apsley Mills and Hemel Hempstead with a steam powered tramway, to feed the Midland line. Berkhamsted was immediately up in arms at the po-tential loss of business, and the promoters hastily offered a branch line scheme between the two towns, via Northchurch, to connect with their tramway at Bourne End.

Lack of funds carried that idea off, and with the railway serving Chesham by 1889 it seemed that was that. Yet in 1900 the scheme was resurrected, this time with electric traction. The Boxmoor Trustees opposed it, and Paston Cooper killed it right off, remarking that he never wanted to go to Chesham and did not see why anyone should want to go.

Meanwhile, on February 9, 1847, the Royal Mail from London was due at 6.25 pm but snow delayed it and the coach drew in at 11.30. Due to the severity of the weather a covey of partridges also arrived, and several took shelter in High street - they were caught.

In 1879 the new horse 'bus service to Berkhamsted cost one shilling if you travelled inside, and saved you 3d if you braved the weather on the outside. Many local people could afford neither, and walked the five miles from Chesham, rather than pay.

In Chesham, Joseph Climpson, carrier was also licensee of the old Waggon and Horses in High street. He held that licence for fifty years. Mail was left at the pub, and farmers from outlying areas would call to collect it. He also carried hay and straw, and his son drove the waggon to London thrice weekly.

Climpson's carriers stayed in the business until 1888-9 when the son disposed of it as the railway neared completion. Young Climpson took the licence of The Huntsman, where the Co-operative Stores now stand, before he moved to the first of two premises in Blucher street where the family have traded ever since, until earlier this year when the town's free vintners closed with the death of Jim Climpson.

Back at the turn of the century, that earlier Climpson still travelled the district, as a wholesale dealer in cigarettes and tobacco. His rounds covered Amersham, Winchmore Hill, Coleshill, Penn Street, both Chalfonts, Fulmer, Denham, Hyde Heath, Lee Common, Ballinger, both Missendens, Prestwood, Wendover, Berkhamsted, Bourne End and Boxmoor!

Finally, an eye witness account of a journey by Climpson's daughter on a local errand: 'Father said "You can drive the horse down Waterside to the Pheasant". I drove in the yard, which had scrubbed tables and benches — and the chickens all flew out the way. Mr Henry Wingrove said "I'm much obliged to you for bringing my order; how much is it?" I told him and he called upstairs to Mrs Wingrove "Emmie, please bring £3.10." Now Father had given me a shilling to say "If you please, Father said would you have a drink?" While I was receipting the invoice, he paid the £3.10 and some change. I drove the horse through Lords Mill stream and gave him a drink, then across The Moor, down Amy lane, King street, Germain street and home; I cashed in, Father thanking me and saying "How like Henry Wingrove only taking for half a pint!" '

As the rail link with London neared completion against its opening in 1889, it was to have stopped short at the Chesham Bois end of the Moor; (hence the Unicorn, or 'Railway Hotel') but public subscription brought it into the town centre, though it never did become a through route running 'in the Vale' on its way 'from Tring to Reigate'. It is often said that Chesham's establishment fought the idea of a through railway, on the premise that if it came at all it must end here, but in fact the many early schemes were set aside in favour of the Euston — Midland line simply because local landowners' opposition was so great. One scheme would have connected Amersham to Wycombe and Chesham to Berkhamsted, but it foundered — 'the only time Tyrwhitt Drakes, Wellers and Earl Howe agreed, was to keep the railway out'.

Stephenson planned a route for his L & NWR from London to Aylesbury via Amersham. Forced to abandon this by the powerful local landowning interests, he turned instead to the route through Berkhamsted, encouraged by the Countess Bridgwater, who suggested he follow the line of the canal across her own land there and at Tring.

It is intriguing to speculate that whichever route was chosen, for whatever reason, Chesham would never have been on a main route anyway, for geographical reasons.

Despite this, the railway brought 4300 people to the town in its first week, which settled to 2,800 in the second. Strangely, outgoing traffic was less at 3000 and 1450. It was reported that the directors took a 'sanguine view' of the new extension of their railway, 'and their opinion is shared by the vast body of shareholders, with an exception here and there.' In September two locals left the town at 6.55 am, took train to London, Dover, and boat to Calais, stayed three hours, and returned the same way to Chesham by 10.38 pm that evening.

Once here, the new railway was not all plain sailing, and by 1892 there were complaints about freight charges. By the end of that year a meeting had been called, and a good many local traders had something to say. It boiled down to the differential between the L & NWR charges from Berkhamsted to town and those from Chesham on the 'Met.' The older route cost 13s 4d per ton of woodware, but the new railway charged 15s 10d.

By the 1920s the emphasis was no longer on rail, but more on roads. On July 7, 1920 the Chesham UDC met and heard evidence of the traffic through the town, and the state of the roads, and decided that it would need more than just a granite chip surface, and more than water spraying to keep the dust down. Tarmac was the answer — 12,000 sq ft of it at between £5000 and £6000 cost, from one end of the town to the other. The motor age was here.

If the movement of goods and people developed new modes, so did the communication of news, opinions and ideas. In the middle of the 19th century, Chesham had no local paper of its own, but simply William Hepburn's *Almanacks.* The earliest surviving annual issues of 1845-8, reporting the previous years, referred to the availability of earlier issues. The *Almanacks* summarised the year's principal events locally; otherwise there was no accessible public record. The first *Almanack* was probably in 1844.

The earliest newspaper in the district was Amersham chemist Broadwater's *Journal,* first a broadsheet, then registered as a newspaper in 1840. Broadwater sold the pharmacy to T. H. King, his son Ebenezer retaining the print shop, and moved the renamed *Buckinghamshire Advertiser* to Uxbridge. In 1880 John King started the rival *Uxbridge Gazette.* Later W. J. Hutchings bought the *Advertiser.*

The *Bucks Examiner* started life in 1889 but twenty one years earlier, on January 4, 1868 there appeared the first issue of the *Chesham Recorder* which incorporated the *Berkhampstead Advertiser,* price one penny. Four pages displayed local advertisements on the front, local news on the back and the then usual 'syndicated' national centre spread inside. The paper was printed and published by T. Leadbeater of High street. Mr Leadbeater was also the town's bookseller and offered 'every description of newspapers, magazines and books at two days' notice'. He apparently continued the *Almanacks,* and would arrange bookbinding, as well as stocking suitable books for gifts. His was a general printing business, supplying local stationery needs, and he would 'advertize' situations vacant for servants at 1s 6d for five lines, charging servants seeking jobs only 1s. He was also agent for bespoke tailors, and carried a stock of readymade garments as an outfitter!

Thus he filled the minds and clothed the bodies of the townspeople.

Mr. Leadbeater's newspaper appears not to have survived many issues, but sometime in 1874, possibly April 26 of that year, Alfred Augustus Holt's The Herts and Bucks Newspaper Company Limited of Town Hall, High street, Berkhamsted (note the change in spelling), printed and published a newspaper in three editions, with common advertising

on the first and fourth pages, and local news in the centre pages. This was *The Chesham News and Advertiser for Herts, Bucks and Beds*, still publishing in 1877. Its companions were the *Tring Telegraph* and *The Berkhamstead Times.*

By 1887 the paper appears to have been reduced to a single edition, with occasional local news inside, overshadowed by national news and syndicated fiction. By this time it was published by Frederick J. King, within the same company, now at Holliday street, Berkhamsted, and was mastheaded somewhat forgettably as *The Berkhamsted Times, Tring Telegraph, Chesham News, and Advertiser for Herts, Bucks and Beds;* price still one penny.

No advertisement was accepted for less than 1s and all advertisements ran through all editions, and were accepted up to Wednesday night for Friday publication. Correspondence was accepted up to Thursday morning but welcomed 'as much earlier as possible.'

Clearly there was now room for an indigenous newspaper, and Chesham had not long to wait. Tradition, the owners and successive editors have originated the *Bucks Examiner* in 1892, Germain street and a local foundation. In fact it was on July 24, 1889 that Messrs Butler & Son of 20 High street, High Wycombe published the first issue of *The Chesham Examiner, Amersham & Rickmansworth Times* from 9, High street, Chesham.

In a portentous, and sometimes pompous leader, the proprietors stated their aims: ' . . . liberty in both thought and speech, in neither licence.' They committed their new paper to 'the tribunal of public opinion' and promised 'facilities for intercommunication . . . a mirror reflecting the progress of the district . . . Public affairs will be minutely and accurately reported . . . ' The paper would 'aim to bring the manufacturer and the merchant, the tradesman and the artizan, the man of business and the man of leisure, the philanthropist and the student in touch each with the other . . . ' The paper warned sternly 'We shall not wear the livery of any party or be fettered by the trammels of any clique.' Finally, 'its promoters venture to hope' for a 'long and intimate connection with the important district from which its name is taken.'

Circulation at the end of the year was claimed to be 1000, and at the same time, Henry Bigg took over No.9. with his thriving drapery business (now Pattersons). Once again words and fashions were tailored on the same premises. By January 1899 the paper had removed to 110 Church street, and was printed and published there by Henry George Bonner, but on July 14, The Chesham Press proudly announced in a leader that it had taken the paper over at its new premises at 16, Germain street. It has been there ever since.

The new proprietors were brisk and to the point with their take-over announcement: 'Another important change has taken place in the life of *The Chesham Examiner* . . . under this new *regime* . . . a very successful career lies before it.' After detailing new plant and premises the new men went on to say ' . . . the influence of *The Examiner* has only been felt in the district immediately surrounding Chesham . . . ' but the company intended 'to record the news of all the towns and villages comprised in the (sic. Amersham) Union.'

The Chesham Examiner ran for 934 issues under this banner, but not without competition. By 1900 it faced two other local competitors.

When the *Chesham Advertiser* first started operations on Saturday, October 22, 1892, J. E. King, "Plain and Artistic Printer and Publisher" announced in his first issue that he had 'fitted up the extensive premises with a COMPLETE PLANT of modern Type and Machinery.' The new paper was published from 7 Red Lion Street, Chesham, and that first issue carried this message from the proprietor: "This being our first issue of the Chesham Advertiser, we would claim indulgence for any shortcomings or oversights . . . although not exactly strange to this busy and friendly little town of Bucks, in business

transactions, until the last few weeks we were comparatively unacquainted."

On October 24, 1900, another *Chesham News* appeared, published by Charles Herbert Peacock of 101 High street and printed by Messrs Smith Bros., newsagents, of 7, Market square - perhaps a response to the six month old takeover of the *Examiner* by the Chesham Press. It survived a mere eight issues, with a final edition of December 12, 1900 announcing a merger with the *West Herts Observer,* due to the conflict of regular local events with press day (!) and the observation that 'our efforts have been to waken up our contemporaries.'

The Chesham Advertiser enjoyed a longer run – until February 28, 1903. What happend to it remains a mystery. There is no evidence here of merger or acquisition, but the *Examiner* does own one of the only known two file copies of the paper's first two years . . . Meanwhile in Uxbridge John King had bought into the other *Advertiser.*

With the opposition safely out of the way, on January 5, 1906, with neither prior nor contemporary announcement, issue no 934 of *The Chesham Examiner* was succeeded by issue no 935 of *The Bucks Examiner.* There were to be further attempts to unseat this powerful little paper. On April 6, 1910 a less parochial *Bucks Recorder* was published by Neil Waud from offices at both 64 Broadway, Chesham and 19 Broadway, Amersham – and printed in north west London. The challenge lasted half as long again as the short lived second *Chesham News,* with a twelfth and last issue on June 22, 1910. W. Pinkham's *Mid-Bucks News,* backed by Conservative Newspapers Ltd., of London and with a claim of 10,000 monthly circulation, only managed one issue.

The *Recorder* at least had some inkling of the problems facing it, and it seems it almost sensed its own brief lifespan. The first issue cautiously commented 'We entered upon the venture . . . with some diffidence. Everybody knows that running a newspaper is an expensive business . . . We have had to experience decided opposition . . . and expect to meet with a good deal more, but we shall fight fair, and trust our opponents to do the same.' The paper stood for Unionism and Tariff Reform, and had the guts to say so – a contrast with the somewhat sickly disclaimers to partiality of all the other contenders. This had obviously caused some comment, as the leader continued 'in refutation of certain malicious statements . . . we have received no help . . . from any Party or individual, in the establishment of the paper.' One's heart warms to Neil Waud when he added 'As a matter of fact, we are risking every brass farthing we possess, and risking it cheerfully. There is nothing like taking the bull by the horns.' He promised concise reports, 'devoid of "padding" ' and anticipated two editions weekly, Wednesdays for South Bucks and Friday for Mid-Bucks. Mr Waud broke new ground too: ' . . . news matter . . . printed on every page tremendously enhances the value of an advertisement. What reader troubles to wade through a solid page of advertisement matter?' Well, Mr Waud was obviously ahead of his time and he paid the penalty, but at least he put Chesham among the pioneers of local newspaper design, and he deserves to be remembered for that and for his sincerity.

Meanwhile in Uxbridge fire destroyed the original 1840 Amersham foundling's premises, the *Buckinghamshire Advertiser* married the *Uxbridge Gazette* in 1916, and later King and Hutchings joined Westminster Press, in turn now within the Longman-Pearson Group.

After World War II, the *Examiner* expanded into Amersham; in 1953 the old *Journal's* successor followed suit. In the mid-50s the *Examiner* echoed the 1870s with its development into Berkhamsted, and today the *Amersham and Chesham Advertiser* edition of the Uxbridge series is based in Amersham, and *The Bucks Examiner* has an Amersham office, while remaining based at Germain street.

THE CHESHAM CONNECTION

Chesham's first newspaper, The Chesham Recorder.

The Chesham News

AND ADVERTISER FOR HERTS, BUCKS AND BEDS.

No. 153   (Registered at the General Post Office as a Newspaper.)   FRIDAY, NOVEMBER 2, 1877   Price ONE PENNY.

ADVERTISE! ADVERTISE!! ADVERTISE!!!

"There is but one way of obtaining business—Publicity ; but one way of obtaining publicity—Advertising."—BLACKWOOD.

"Advertising is to business what Steam is to Machinery—the grand propelling power."—MACAULAY.

"The Berkhamsted Times,"
Published every Saturday.

"The Chesham News,"
Published every Friday.

"The Tring Telegraph,"
Published every Friday.

All Advertisements appear in the three Papers for a single fee ; thus giving advertisers an advantage not offered by any other paper in the two counties of Herts and Bucks.

Advertising gives impetus to trade, and tact holds the helm. As a matter of experience, it is beyond dispute that judicious advertising pays to an extent beyond any ordinary comparison with its cost. The progress of competition is so rapid that a "good old house" which does not advertise is in danger of losing much sound custom. Some people think it *smacks* of dignity to say they can live without advertising. They may *live* upon this kind of dignity ; but life is one thing and success in life is another. A good reputation in business means that you shall be *widely* as well as favourably known. A good advertisement in a widely circulated newspaper is the best of all possible salesmen. It is a salesman who never sleeps and is never weary ; who goes after business early and late, who accosts the merchant in his shop, the scholar in his study, the lawyer in his office, the lady at her breakfast-table, and the public everywhere.

ABOVE LEFT: The masthead of the town's second newspaper, The Chesham News, and BELOW: the proprietor's faith in the power of advertising, 1877. ABOVE CENTRE: The Chesham Connection – to Berkhamsted and BELOW: the smithy in Broadway, next to the Independent Chapel. ABOVE RIGHT: The Chesham Railway Coach (L & NWR horse 'bus) on its way from Berkhamsted, in the Hockeridges, 1880s. (CM/PB) and BELOW: Gooding's forge in Germain street, where the car park access now lies.

LEFT: Foden waggon and trailer hauling freight between Berkhamsted and Chesham in 1910 (JPM), and RIGHT: cutting the chalk for Chesham's new railway. BELOW: The 'Met' arrives at Chesham in 1889.

The Chesham News.

No. 1.   Wednesday, October 24. 1900.   One Half penny.

MID BUCKS EDITION.

The Bucks Recorder

WITH WHICH IS INCORPORATED

The Amersham Mail and South Bucks Recorder.

Circulating throughout the whole of the Parliamentary Divisions of Mid Bucks & South Bucks.

WEDNESDAY, APRIL 6TH, 1910.

The
Mid=Bucks.
News

Circulating in
Aylesbury, Great Missenden, Amersham, Chesham, etc. etc.

OCTOBER, 1929.

*ABOVE: Staff and steam at Chesham Station, and
BELOW: The masthead of the shortlived Chesham News,
October 24, 1900, of the even shorter lived Bucks
Recorder, April 6, 1910 and the shortest lived of them
all, the Mid-Bucks News of October 1929. (NL)*

The Chesham Examiner,
AMERSHAM & RICKMANSWORTH TIMES.

NO. 1. VOL. 1.   CHESHAM, WEDNESDAY, JULY 24, 1889.   ONE PENNY.

DIX AND Co.,

WHOLESALE & BUILDERS'

IRONMONGERS,

IRON, STEEL, LEAD, OIL & COLOR MERCHANTS,

HIGH WYCOMBE.

BUILDERS, SMITHS, WHEELWRIGHTS, & THE TRADE SUPPLIED AT WHOLESALE PRICES.

PROMPT DELIVERY FROM STOCK.

HOUSE FURNISHING IN ALL ITS BRANCHES
AT THE OLD ESTABLISHED
FURNISHING WAREHOUSE,
OF FORTY YEARS' STANDING, IN
GERMAIN STREET, CHESHAM,
CARRIED ON BY
G. FREEMAN AND SONS,
WHO ARE PREPARED TO GIVE ESTIMATES FOR

HOUSE FURNISHING from 50 to 2,000 GUINEAS.
BEDROOM SUITES from £1 18s. to 100 GUINEAS
DINING and DRAWING ROOM SUITES from 5 to 50 GUINEAS
A LARGE STOCK of BEDSTEADS from 10s. to 50 GUINEAS

FURNITURE REMOVED BY ROAD OR RAIL.

AUCTIONS, ESTATE AGENCIES AND VALUATIONS carried out and Settlements made with promptness and dispatch.

VISIT OF THE SHAH TO ASHRIDGE.

PHOTOGRAPHS OR GROUPS
TAINING PORTRAITS OF

THE SHAH OF PERSIA
AND SUITE.

PRINCE ALBERT VICTOR,

EARL & COUNTESS BROWNLOW,
&c.

ON SALE

PRICE 2s. and 2s. 6d. EACH

WILLIAM COLES,
PHOTOGRAPHER.

WATFORD & CHESHAM

CHARLES LONG,
Wholesale Boot and Shoe Manufacturer, and
Leather and Grindery Merchant,

BROADWAY.

CHESHAM.

Specialities—Strong Tipped and Hobbed Navvy Watertights, Keepers', Shooters', Derbys', Rifles, &c.

RIVETTED & HANDSEWN.

Trial Orders Solicited.

SAMPLES SENT ON APPROVAL

SALMON'S READING TEA.

STATION WORKS.

OPPOSITE PASSENGER STATION

Cheap Depot for all kinds of Building Materials.

SPECIAL PRICES QUOTED FOR TRUCK LOADS.

C. H. HUNT,
STATION WORKS, HIGH WYCOMBE

SEASONABLE QUESTIONS.

Do want a Good Tricycle?
Do you want a Cheap Bicycle?
Do you want easy Terms?

SENSIBLE ADVICE:
TRY
GEORGE NEALE,
IRONMONGER,

HIGH STREET, CHESHAM

WE ARE
ALMOST UNKNOWN
IN CENTRAL AFRICA.

YES! EVEN

G. J. & A. SMITH,

BOOKSELLERS,

STATIONERS,
AND
NEWSAGENTS,

108, CHURCH STREET,
CHESHAM.

Books for Prizes and Birthday Presents.

Bibles and Prayer Books in various Styles and Bindings.

A large selection of Hymn Books, including

"SACRED SONGS AND SOLOS"

HYMNAL COMPANION.

CHURCH HYMNS,

HYMNS ANCIENT AND MODERN,

PSALMS AND HYMNS WITH SUPPLEMENT.

MISSION HYMNAL, &c.

Depot for the Religious Tract Society's Books and Magazines.

Partridge & Co.'s Cheap "Pansy" series and other publications.

HORNER'S PENNY STORIES ALWAYS IN STOCK.

Morning Papers for breakfast.
Evening Papers by Fast Evening Train. Every effort made to insure the latest possible Edition.

BOOKBINDING AT LONDON PRICES.

MISCELLANEOUS ORDERS EXECUTED WITH DESPATCH.

Established 1854.

WILLIAM G. HARDING,
Builder & Undertaker,
FURNISHING & GENERAL IRONMONGER, CUTLER, &c.
BROADWAY, HIGH STREET,
CHESHAM, BUCKS.
FUNERALS CONDUCTED THROUGHOUT
Wire Blinds made to order.   Repairs neatly executed.

Visitors to Chesham who require refreshment should do well to try

WM. IVORY,
Cosy Nook Coffee Tavern,
HIGH STREET, CHESHAM.

Open daily.   (Sundays excepted)
TEA AND COFFEE ALWAYS READY.
CHARLES BOOKSELLE,

Daily and Evening Papers on Sale.

Orders taken on behalf of G. J. and A. Smith, Church Street, for all kinds of Stationery, Periodicals, Through subscriptions.

DEAN'S
COUGH MIXTURE.
A combination of Linseed, Aniseed, Ipecac, Tolu, &c.

C. G. DEAN, M.P.S.
CHEMIST, &c.,
High Street, Chesham.
ESTABLISHED 1864
Agent to the SUN FIRE AND LIFE OFFICE

DEAN'S
VEGETABLE
RESTORATIVE PILLS.

DIRECTIONS

C. G. DEAN, M.P.S.
Chemist, &c.,
High Street, Chesham.

CHESHAM—

Every THURSDAY, at Mr. PIGGIN'S, High Street, from 11 o'clock to 4

HIGH WYCOMBE
DENTAL SURGERY.

MR. EDWARD MAWER,
THE OLD-ESTABLISHED
RESIDENT
SURGEON DENTIST,
DAILY ATTENDANCE AT
8, HIGH STREET,
HIGH WYCOMBE.

Mr. MAWER begs to state that owing to increasing work at home, he is quite unable to attend personally at the several towns around where he has Branch Establishments, but his Colleague will visit those regularly as announced.

Mr. MAWER is at home daily at No. 8, High-street, High Wycombe, where he may be consulted on all matters pertaining to Dentistry.

ADVICE & CONSULTATION FREE.

ARTIFICIAL
TEETH.

ARTIFICIAL
TEETH.

MR. MAWER,
HIGH WYCOMBE

WILLESDEN, HARROW, UXBRIDGE, RICKMANSWORTH, CHESHAM, AYLESBURY, VERNEY JUNCTION & BRILL.

DOWN TRAINS—WEEK DAYS.

	a.m.	a.m.	a.m.	a.m.	a.m.	a.m.	a.m.	a.m.	a.m.	a.m.	a.m.	a.m.	a.m.	a.m.	a.m.	a.m.	a.m.	a.m.	a.m.	a.m.	a.m.	a.m.	a.m. PR	a.m.	a.m. H	a.m.	a.m.	a.m.	a.m.	a.m.	a.m.	a.m.
BAKER ST. ...dep.	...	5 20	...	5 35	5 50	6 0	6 5	6 10	6 20	...	6 30	...	6 40	6 50	...	7 0	7 5	7 15	7 20	7 25	7 27	7 30	7 35	7 40	7 45	7 47	7 50	7 55	7 58	8 1	...	8 5	8 8
St. John's Wood Rd. ,,	...	5 22	...	5 37	5 52	6 2	...	6 12	6 22	...	6 32	...	...	...	...	...	7 7	7 17	7 22	7 27	7 29	7 32	7 37	7 42	7 47	7 49	7 52	7 57	8 0	8 3	...	8 7	8 10
Marlborough Rd. ,,	...	5 24	...	5 39	5 54	6 4	...	6 14	6 24	...	6 34	...	...	...	...	...	6 54	7 19	7 24	7 29	7 31	7 34	7 39	7 44	7 49	7 51	7 54	7 59	8 2	8 5	...	8 9	8 12
Swiss Cottage ,,	...	5 26	...	5 41	5 56	6 6	6 11	6 16	6 26	...	6 38	...	...	...	...	7 3	7 17	7 21	7 26	7 31	7 33	7 36	7 41	7 46	7 51	...	7 56	8 1	8 4	8 7	...	8 11	8 14
Finchley Road ...	...	5 28	...	5 43	5 58	6 8	6 13	6 18	6 28	...	6 38	...	...	...	...	6 8	7 8	7 23	7 26	7 37	7 35	7 38	7 43	7 48	7 53	7 55	7 58	8 3	8 6	8 9	...	8 13	8 16
West Hampstead	...	5 30	...	5 45	6 0	6 10	6 15	6 20	6 30	...	6 40	...	...	...	...	6 10	7 0	7 25	7 30	7 37	7 35	7 40	7 45	7 50	7 55	7 57	8 0	8 5	8 8	8 11	...	8 15	8 18
Kilburn-Brondsb'y ,,	...	5 32	...	5 47	6 2	6 12	6 17	6 22	6 32	...	6 42	...	...	...	...	6 27	2	7 27	7 32	7 37	7 37	7 42	7 47	7 52	7 57	7 59	2	7 8	10 8	13	...	8 17	8 20
WILLESDEN G'N &...	...	5 34	...	5 49	6 4	6 14	6 19	6 24	6 34	...	6 44	...	...	...	...	6 4	4	7 29	7 34	7 39	7 39	7 44	7 49	7 54	7 59	8 1	3	8 5	9	8 15	...	819	822
CRICKLEWOOD	...	...	...	...	...	...	...	...	6 47	...	6 47	...	...	...	...	7 7	7	7 32	7 34	7 42	7 42	7 47	7 52	7 57	8 18	8 6	8 18	...	...	8 18	...	...	...
Kingsb'ry-Neasden ,,	5 7	5 37	...	5 52	6 7	...	...	6 22	...	...	...	...	...	...	...	7 0	7 22	7 32	...	...	...	7 47	...	...	...	...	8 22	...	...	...	...	...	...
Wembley Park ... ,,	...	5 40	...	...	6 10	...	...	6 40	...	...	...	...	...	...	7 25	7 35	7 25	7 35	...	7 45	...	...	...	...	8 9	...	8 25	...	...	...	...	...	...
MARYLEBONE ,,	...	...	5 35	...	...	...	...	6 50	...	...	...	6 50	...	...	...	7 35	7 35	7 41	...	7 51	...	...	...	...	8 15	8 9	8 18	...	8 5	...	...	8 31	...
Harrow-on-the-Hill ,,	5 15	5 46	5 52	616	635	6 52	6 55	7	7 6	716	7	5 27	7 15	8 7	731	...	...	8 2	8 21	8 0	...	...	...	...	7 48	7 34	...	...	8 22	...	...	...	...
§ UXBRIDGE { arr.	615	...	...	...	656	6 20	716	739	...	...	...	7 30	...	8 2	...	8 21	...	8 19	...	...	...	...	...	...	7 48	7 48	...	...	7 48	...	...	...	...
{ dep.	...	5 39	5 57	6 32	...	6 20	6 57	...	...	...	...	...	...	...	...	...	...	...	...	...	...	...	...	...	8 19	8 27	...	...	8 27	...	...	...	...
Pinner ... ...dep.	...	...	6 2	6 37	...	7 2	7 16	...	...	...	752	...	...	8 6	...	...	...	8 24	...	...	...	...	...	...	8 24	8 32	...	...	8 32	...	...	...	...
Northwood ,, ,,	...	...	6 10	6 44	...	7 8	7 24	...	...	...	...	...	...	...	...	...	...	8 31	...	...	...	...	...	...	8 31	8 37	...	...	8 40	...	...	...	...
Rickmansworth ,, ,,	...	...	6 15	6 50	...	...	...	...	...	...	...	...	...	...	...	744	...	...	...	...	...	...	...	...	8 37	8 45	...	...	8 46	...	...	...	...
Chorley Wood ... ,,	...	...	...	6 56	...	...	...	...	...	...	...	8 16	...	...	...	753	...	...	...	...	...	...	...	...	8 45	...	...	...	8 53	...	...	...	...
CHALFONT ROAD { arr.	...	...	...	7 9	...	...	...	...	...	...	...	8 25	...	...	...	...	...	...	...	...	...	...	...	...	...	...	...	...	9 2	...	...	...	...
CHESHAM { arr.	...	...	...	7 20	...	...	...	...	...	812	...	...	...	...	...	...	...	8 35	...	...	...	...	...	...	8 35	...	...	...	...	...	...	...	...
{ dep.	...	...	...	7 2	...	...	...	7 37	...	...	...	...	...	...	...	...	...	8 50	...	...	...	...	...	...	8 50	...	...	...	...	...	...	...	...
Amersham ...dep.	...	...	...	7 11	...	...	...	7 46	...	...	...	...	...	...	...	...	...	8 59	...	...	...	...	...	...	8 59	...	...	...	...	...	...	...	...
Great Missenden	...	...	...	7 19	...	...	...	...	...	...	...	...	...	...	...	...	...	9 7	...	...	...	...	...	...	9 7	...	...	...	...	...	...	...	...
Wendover... ... ,,	...	...	...	7 24	...	...	...	7 57	...	...	...	...	...	...	...	...	...	9 12	...	...	...	...	...	...	9 12	...	...	...	...	...	...	...	...
Stoke Mandeville ,,	...	...	...	7 29	...	...	...	8 2	...	...	...	...	...	...	...	...	...	9 17	...	...	...	...	...	...	9 17	...	...	...	...	...	...	...	...
AYLESBURY { arr.	6 40	...	...	7 31	...	...	...	8 4	...	...	...	...	...	...	...	...	...	9 18	...	...	...	...	...	...	9 18	...	...	...	...	...	...	...	...
{ dep.	6 51	...	...	7 40	...	8 5	...	8 12	...	...	...	...	...	...	...	...	...	...	...	...	...	...	...	...	9 27	...	...	...	...	...	...	...	...
Waddesdon Manor ,,	6 55	...	...	7 44	...	816	...	8 16	...	...	...	...	...	...	...	...	...	...	...	...	...	...	...	...	9 31	...	...	...	...	...	...	...	...
Quainton Road ,,	7 6	...	...	...	...	816	...	To	...	...	...	...	...	...	...	...	...	...	...	...	...	...	...	...	...	...	...	...	...	...	...	...	...
GrandboroughRoad,,	7 11	...	...	...	...	8 21	...	Leicester	...	...	...	...	...	...	...	...	...	...	...	...	...	...	...	...	...	...	...	...	...	...	...	...	...
Winslow Road ,,	7 15	...	...	...	...	826	...	...	...	...	...	...	...	...	...	...	...	...	...	...	...	...	...	...	...	...	...	...	...	...	...	...	...
VERNEY JUNC. arr.	7 15	...	...	...	...	826	...	...	...	...	...	...	...	...	...	...	...	...	...	...	...	...	...	...	...	...	...	...	...	...	...	...	...

* Passengers wishing to alight at Westcott and Wood Siding Stations should inform the Guard at the previous Station, the train will also call at these Stations as required to take up passengers.
Trains do not stop at Stations marked thus — H Horse and Carriage traffic is not conveyed by Trains marked thus H
§ All Trains also stop at Rayners Lane, Eastcote, Ruislip and Ickenham in both directions. †Change at Northwood and Aylesbury. P R These Trains will stop at Preston Road to set down Passengers on notice being given to the Guard at the previous stopping place, and to pick up Passengers on notice being given at Preston Road.

OXFORD AND AYLESBURY TRAMWAY SERVICE.					
To BRILL.	8.0				
	a.m.	a.m.	p.m.	p.m.	p.m.
BAKER ST. dep.	7 45	9 45	220	5 10	715
AYLESBURY ,,	9 18	1145	350	623	9 1
Verney Jc., ,,	8 45	1060	330	6 0	7 0
Quainton Rd., ,,	9 35	12 6	4 86	42	920
Waddesdon ,,	9 44	1214	416	50	928
Westcott * ,,	*	*	*	*	*
Wotton ,,	9 57	1227	429	7	941
Wood Sdg. *,,	*	*	*	*	*
BRILL ...... arr.	1013	1245	445	7 19	957

Part of the June 1909 Metropolitan Railway Time Table for the Chesham commuter. (DJN)

ABOVE: Mr Grace's coal cart calls, and CENTRE: private transport on Eskdale avenue, while BELOW: Sunday cart washing is nothing new – at Town Bridge.

128

*ABOVE: An outing flies the flag, followed by everyday
transport in High street outside Chapter One bookshop,
while LEFT: Mr Woodley (after whose father, John, Woodley
Hill was named) provided a local carrier's service, (IN)
and RIGHT: later outings went by charabanc from the
Broadway.*

129

ABOVE: The gateway to the town outside Amy Mill House was less trafficked when these early cyclists set off, and BELOW: when motor transport eventually took over, congestion, like this at Red Lion street corner, was the beginning of the end of the old Chesham.

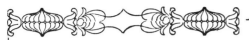

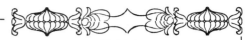

INDEX

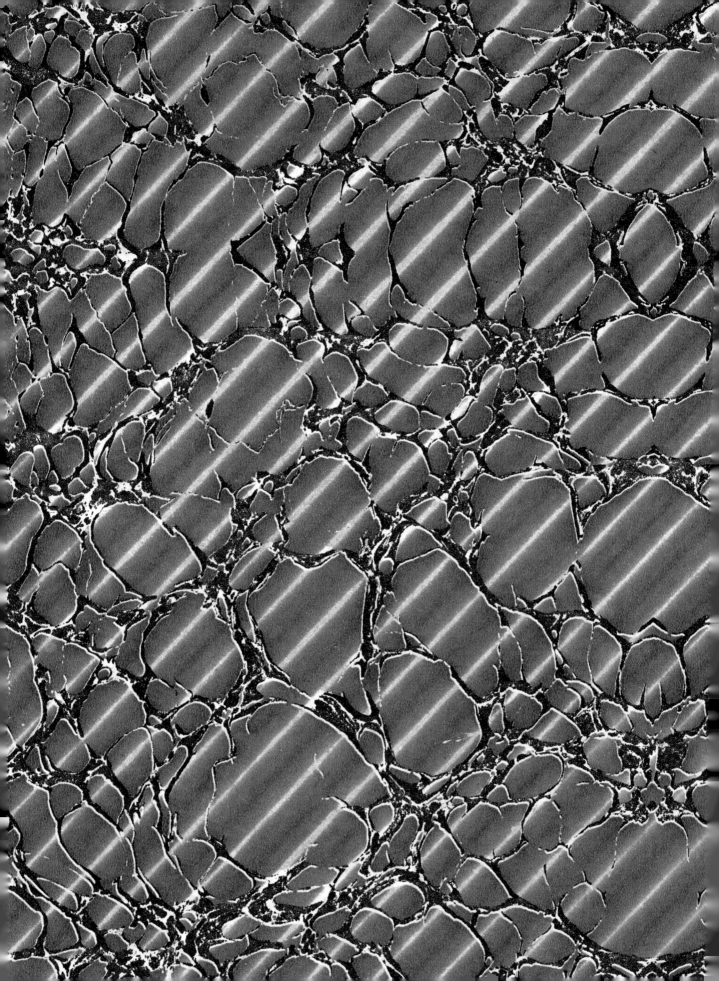